The Accidental Addict

Di Porritt was born in Melbourne in 1938. She is a company director, and was a successful businesswoman for over twenty years. She is married with three children, and lives in Melbourne.

Di Russell was born in Sydney in 1948. Her family later moved to Victoria. She has a Master of Arts from the University of Melbourne. She teaches Literature and Communication at RMIT, and lives in Melbourne.

DI PORRITT & DI RUSSELL

The
ACCIDENTAL ADDICT

PAN
AUSTRALIA

This book is dedicated to the memory
of Maurice Payne and
Helen and Hugh Robertson

First published in Pan by Pan Macmillan Publishers Australia 1994
a division of Pan Macmillan Australia Pty Limited
63-71 Balfour Street, Chippendale, Sydney

National Library of Australia
cataloguing-in-publication data:

Porritt, Di
The accidental addict.

ISBN 0 330 35593 7.

1. Benzodiazepine abuse. 2. Medication abuse. I. Russell, Di. II. Title

613.8

Typeset in 10/12 Cheltenham by Midland Typesetters, Maryborough
Printed in Australia by McPherson's Print Group, Maryborough

Contents

Acknowledgements

This book could not have been written without the courage and generosity of fifty people who gave us hours of their time, talked frankly about private matters, and endured follow-up phone calls – often when they were unwell. Twenty health professionals also spoke to us at length. We sincerely thank them all.

The Melbourne agency TRANX has helped many people to identify their illness and come off their pills. We would like to thank the staff for their tireless work in bringing the serious problem of benzodiazepine addiction to the notice of the public.

We are indebted to the staff of the former Women's Health Resource Collective: Debbie Milligan, Vicki McLean, Mirella Marini, Juliane Carey and Barbara Younger. They auspiced our submissions for funding and provided us with a small office. Their kindness and good humour created a warm and supportive working environment. Particular thanks to Nancy Peck for her help with submission writing.

Our gratitude to John and Margaret Howard, Linda Bowen, and Rina Cruickshank for their help and support.

Thanks to Don Porritt for his help with

computer problems, to Paul Byrne, Jenny Pausacker, and Alan Porritt for their help with research, their faith in the project and their wise counsel. Sandy Fitts gave us some perceptive advice about the format of the book. Thanks also to our editor, Michael Langley.

The research for this book was funded by Consumers' Health Forum and the Lance Reichstein Foundation.

Special thanks to Will Day, who was a member of our team for more than three years and participated equally in the research. Will's intelligence, enthusiasm and excellent interviewing skills were highly valued and contributed to the success of the project.

Preface

Many Australians through no fault of their own have become 'accidental addicts' – unwittingly addicted to and sickened by their prescribed doses of sleeping pills, minor tranquillisers or muscle relaxants. They are not irresponsible 'pill-poppers', but average men and women encountering the day-to-day troubles of life. Their only mistake is that they obediently take their medication.

Although benzodiazepines (the name of the chemical used for these drugs) can be very helpful as a short-term support, they have ruined careers and disrupted lives when taken over a long period. Recent government guidelines recommend that benzodiazepine prescriptions be restricted to between two and four weeks, and that people who take benzodiazepines on a long-term basis should be carefully monitored. However, millions of prescriptions continue to be written each year and too many people are still becoming addicted.

We first became friends at TRANX, a Melbourne tranquilliser rehabilitation agency, while working as volunteer telephone counsellors and support-group organisers. So many of the people we talked to then, in the late 1980s, were very sick indeed – and for much longer than they anticipated. Despite the sensational 'Valium Addict' features which regularly appeared in the media, there was not enough information available about the protracted illness benzos can cause. Over and over again in support groups and on the telephone we heard the comment, 'Someone should write a book about this.'

In 1990 we established the Benzodiazepine Research Group and, with funding from the Consumers' Health Forum and the Lance Reichstein Foundation, spent three years researching the experiences of people suffering from the effects of benzos. The result is *The Accidental Addict*, culled from fifty formal interviews (and hundreds of telephone counselling sessions). We believe the personal testimonies gathered here clearly establish the extent of the damage – physical and psychological – caused by benzodiazepines.

The Accidental Addict portrays the lives of men and women who have overcome benzo addiction and rediscovered life. It tells their stories in their own words. It also includes a comprehensive description of benzo symptoms, as well as an evaluation of the various therapies people tried.

We believe this information will comfort and reassure people going through benzo withdrawal. We also want to reach others who are worried that they may be addicted – perhaps they have tried to come off before, failed and now blame themselves. Because benzo sickness and addiction has a habit of sneaking up on people, those who don't recognise how their health has been affected are in fact a much larger group at risk – they have yet to make the connection between their ailment and their drug.

And then there are those who believe it won't happen to them, not on their tiny dose – just one sleeping tablet before bed . . .

The Accidental Addict is also intended as a book for carers, those on the outside of benzo sickness – those who love someone affected by benzos, or those who think someone they know may be affected: the woman who is concerned that her mother is gulping down too many pills but is still as sick – if not sicker – than ever; the wife worried about her husband who starts each day with a tranquilliser because he feels he can't keep up with his job. Health professionals – doctors, nurses, counsellors – are also in the front line of dealing with benzo withdrawal. Because benzo sickness is not a 'proper' illness – it has no well-known list of symptoms in medical books – *The Accidental Addict* is designed to provide health professionals with a comprehensive overview of the experiences and symptoms of benzo sufferers.

We believe this book will provide inspiration and encouragement for people withdrawing from benzodiazepines. However, it is not intended to be a self-help book, which is why we have not included guidelines or instructions for dosage reductions. If, after reading *The Accidental Addict*, you decide to come off your pills, it is important that you contact an appropriate health professional. Withdrawal symptoms affect people in many ways, some of which can seriously incapacitate them. A list of drug rehabilitation agencies can be found in the White Pages of your local telephone directory.

Di Porritt and Di Russell

How Benzodiazepines Affect the Brain

Benzodiazepines cause very profound alterations in the brain's biochemistry. When absorbed through the body's systems, they magnify the action of the brain's receptors – the brain's own natural tranquilliser. Receptors help to calm down the brain and decrease the body's responses and emotions. Benzodiazepines, however, exaggerate all these actions, causing a general damping down of emotional responses, memory and arousal.

When people take benzodiazepines long-term, the brain decides that it has no need for its normal number of receptors, and starts to destroy them. The brain then becomes drug dependent and more benzodiazepines are needed to make people feel normal. If the dose is not increased, people start to experience withdrawal symptoms, both emotional and physical. Some of these are anxiety, depression, mental confusion, fearfulness, severe headaches, and digestive problems.

For people to get well, the brain needs to experience a period when the level of the drug is progressively reduced, until it is entirely absent.

Further time is required for the brain to manufacture the additional receptors needed to function normally again. This time varies from person to person.

Introduction – The Benzo Business

Human beings have always sought relief from stress, anxiety and sleeplessness. Benzodiazepines, first released in the early 1960s, were the latest in a long line of drugs that claimed to promote tranquillity and sound sleep. They became one of the most successful drugs ever produced. The reason for this success is simple: their target market was just about everybody. They were handed out for bereavement, divorce, running a home, raising a family, examination nerves, stomach trouble, headaches, overwork – the list is endless. As one early advertising slogan for a brand of benzos put it: 'Whatever the diagnosis – Librium.' Healthy people were routinely put on these drugs to help them deal with the ordinary problems of life.

The idea that life is a condition which needs drug therapy would have seemed very odd fifty years ago. Our grandparents were no strangers to anxiety and stress – after all, they lived through the Depression and two world wars. But the virtues of stoicism and fortitude were more highly valued then. When kids were miserable at school, when they fell over and hurt their knee, they were told to 'grin and bear it'. If someone asked how you were, you probably responded, 'Well, mustn't complain.'

Conditions might have been tough for most people in those days, but family ties were stronger and communities more close-knit. Friends and neighbours were there to see you through, and the local vicar was available to talk things over. When things went wrong, a good strong cup of tea or a stiff drink were the most likely prescriptions.

After the war, Australian society changed dramatically. Our living standards rose rapidly and mass markets were developed. The very last thing manufacturers and businesses wanted was a population sitting at home stoically enduring their suffering. They wanted active, impatient consumers who expected instant gratification – a quick fix. Our values had to be changed. Advertising, particularly through television, brought images of smiling people living perfect lives right into our homes. And if those blissfully happy people were normal, it was possible to regard the stress and pain which are part of the human condition as abnormal. If a *problem* could be defined as an *illness*, then it made sense to design and market a medicine to treat it.

But the widespread distribution of drugs on a long-term basis costs a lot of money. There has always been some prescribing of mood-altering drugs such as morphine and cocaine to relieve pain, and barbiturates were used as tranquillisers and sleeping pills. But before the war it would have been economically unthinkable for a large percentage of the population to be put on medication for anxiety or insomnia. Poorer people could barely afford to see a doctor, and drugs were expensive. But in the 1960s, Australia's new prosperity meant that it was possible for the state to subsidise drugs, and at the same time higher individual incomes meant that large numbers of people could afford to use a long-term medication to help them 'cope' with life. We were ready for a 'happy pill', and we had the money to pay for it. The stage was set for benzodiazepines.

When Librium and Valium – the first benzodiazepines – were released, they were marketed as wonder drugs, non-addictive, with virtually no side-effects. Benzos, it was claimed, could tranquillise without sedating – patients would be left calm but alert. To emphasise that benzos were intended for small-scale problems rather than serious mental illness, they were referred to for many years as 'minor' tranquillisers. The name also seemed to suggest that benzos were mild and safe – almost like a glass of warm milk – compared to other mood-altering drugs. Certainly they were safer than barbiturates, which had always carried a high risk of fatal overdose. They quickly replaced barbiturates, particularly after they were made available under the Pharmaceutical Benefits Scheme in 1973.

Drug companies developed many new brands, marketing them aggressively to doctors. Through their advertising and promotion in medical journals they have great power to influence prescribing habits. Benzodiazepines became one of the most commonly prescribed drugs in Australia. Many of the people who were prescribed these drugs in the 1960s and '70s continue to be addicted to them – and new recruits are still being added to their ranks.

Insomnia

One of the most common reasons for prescribing benzodiazepines is as sleeping pills. Temazepam, issued as Euhypnos or Normison, is the third most prescribed drug in Australia. Mogadon, probably the best known, is almost an institution, and has the status of a benign old favourite, familiarised by its nickname, 'Moggies'. Indeed some people think that sleeping pills are not really benzos, but somehow safer, something like a mug of Milo in a pill. People will often say, 'Well, I got off those dreadful tranquillisers; now I'm just taking my sleeping pills.'

Anxiety

It is often thought that people who are given benzos must be nervous types, somehow temperamentally or biochemically more anxious than the norm. Some studies claim that this is so, arguing that so-called 'passive dependent' personalities – clinging vines who need a prop – are more likely candidates for tranquillisers. But like all attempts to generalise about human 'types', this is doubtful. The trouble is that it's hard to judge whether people are born anxious or made anxious by their circumstances. But the two groups put together make up an enormous number of consumers: a very substantial target market.

Life crisis

The one thing we can be sure of is that nothing is sure. A woman's husband suddenly leaves her and walks out with somebody else. A love affair is abruptly ended. A young person is sexually assaulted. A spouse dies after many years of secure and comfortable marriage. Against expectation a worker is retrenched. Human life is full of pain and difficulty, and clever drug companies have turned this into a marketing angle for their products. For many years pharmaceutical company advertising reinforced the idea that benzodiazepines provided an appropriate solution to problems of trauma and grief. It was also common to prescribe them – inappropriately – for depression. Although this is less frequent now, it still happens.

In the short term – for a few days – benzos do provide a respite from pain or a few nights' sleep. Too often, however, this turns into long-term use. Distraught patients who consult a doctor with symptoms caused by life crisis may walk out clutching a prescription for benzos – perhaps the beginning of years of addiction. Recalling that first prescription, many people have reflected that it took them far longer to recover from the effects of benzodiazepines than from the original problem.

Mother's Little Helper

Ingenious drug company marketing created a wide range of characters and situations suitable for benzo treatment. In the early days, during the 1960s and early '70s, advertisers concentrated most of their energies on a particular target: women.

If asked to do a thumbnail sketch of the kind of person most likely to be prescribed benzos, most people would probably even now respond with a portrait of a neurotic housewife – that object of mockery in the Rolling Stones' song 'Mother's Little Helper'. She is so hopeless that she has to gulp down four more of her little yellow pills as soon as she leaves the doctor's surgery. It is a cruel picture, but it has the power to capture the imagination. The lyrics reinforce the perception that women are nervy and hysterical and therefore need calming medication. Photographs in medical journals of the time showed women clutching brooms or hunched over ironing boards with tousled hair and a look of frenzy, apparently about to fall apart because they could not press the creases right. These images made fools of women by suggesting that even simple household tasks were beyond them.

Nevertheless, the marketing campaigns were frighteningly effective. Women become stressed because they face so many conflicting demands as wives and mothers. They run households, often supporting dependent children and ageing parents. They may be trapped in bad or even violent marriages.

As the 1970s wore on, the profile of women changed as further roles were added. Women were increasingly likely to be in paid jobs as well as maintaining their household duties. Migrant women, subject to all of these pressures as well as having to learn a new language, were particularly vulnerable. Instead of the social and family support they needed, millions of women were handed out benzos: two-thirds of all prescriptions issued.

Men – the forgotten third

Although drug companies focused on women, they did not ignore the potential of men as a market. While popular stereotypes belittle women and make them seem less than they are, such images tend to inflate men and suggest that they should be more than they are. This creates its own set of problems. Very few ordinary men can hope to live up to the image of a perfect male in our society: the successful professional/wise husband and father/provider of an affluent lifestyle for his wife and children. The gap between the ideal and reality leaves men vulnerable to emotional distress when they do not measure up as achievers, husbands, lovers or fathers, and so they too are prescribed benzodiazepines.

One-third of all prescriptions for benzos are issued to males. People are often surprised by this statistic – partly because of another favourite stereotype: it is not socially approved for 'real men' to resort to pills when they are in trouble. Ironically, alcohol is more acceptable. So strong is this idea that men who develop problems with benzos are sometimes ashamed to seek help. A counsellor at a Melbourne drug support agency tells of a man who insisted that he could only come for an interview after dark. He questioned her very closely about the streetscape surrounding the building – could he approach without being spotted? He was scared that the truth about his 'effeminate' problem would be discovered by his workmates.

Men are prescribed benzos for many reasons, often but not always to do with work stress. Once again drug companies pitched their marketing campaigns at a specific stereotype: the business executive. Advertisements in medical journals showed scenes of an anxious managing director facing a nasty situation in the boardroom. Work stress is not confined to high-flying executives, male or female. If you work long hours, if you do shift work, if you take a second job, if you have a demanding occupation at whatever level, from barrister to ambulance officer, then you are vulnerable to the symptoms of nervous exhaustion and stress. In particular, you risk suffering a panic attack, one of the most frightening of all human experiences – and one which often leads to a first prescription for benzos.

> I was on the night train to Sydney, on a business trip. I went to bed and in the morning I had the most awful panic attack. It was a terrifying feeling of palpitations, rather like a tap that was turned on slowly and then suddenly turned on more and more. It welled up into fierce palpitations, leaving me feeling faint and giddy and sick. I was sure I was about to snuff it. At the time I thought it was some physical symptom – I didn't link it with stress.

A sudden panic attack can shake you to the core, particularly as it usually strikes so abruptly out of the blue. But terrifying as they are, panic attacks do not mean that a person is sick. They are a normal response to stress – a warning signal that the mind and body are being placed under too much pressure in a life situation which needs resolution, not a bottle of tranquillisers.

Physical aches and pains

During the 1970s, women's groups in the community began to protest at the relentless targeting of women by the drug companies. As their campaigns started to bite, marketers began to search for new avenues of benzo use. One of these was to promote prescription for physical ailments. Benzos are a muscle relaxant, which gives them a multitude of uses in sports medicine, for shin splints and muscle cramps. Dentists issued prescriptions for jaw and other related pains. Benzos were routinely given to paraplegics for muscle spasm. Menstrual problems provided further retail opportunities: cramps, PMT, hot flushes and other menopausal symptoms. Anything with a stress or muscular tension aspect was a benzo 'opportunity': stomach upsets, bowel problems, migraines. One woman was prescribed benzos for a flickering eye; she was told it was a medicine designed specifically to cure her problem.

If people in this group go on to develop dependency problems with the drugs, it is not surprising that they resist any attempt to classify them as 'chronically anxious to start with' – that favourite benzo stereotype. Often they emphasise how robust their mental and physical health was before they became dependent on benzodiazepines.

The elderly

Elderly people became another key target market for the drug companies. The mere fact of being old is increasingly seen as an unfortunate condition in our society. The youth culture created in the 1960s was partly responsible for this shift in perception. Advertising agencies and the media became obsessed with lithe young bodies and smooth skins to sell products, so that wisdom and experience, the attributes of age, were not much valued any more. Old people began to lose respect and to become invisible – except to the drug companies.

Ever alert, drug companies saw a marketing niche in those unwanted citizens. Doctors were urged to prescribe benzos for the relief of 'excessive geriatric anxiety' for elderly people who could not cope so well with life because they were losing their faculties, because they were lonely or because they were living in reduced circumstances. In the 1970s and '80s, there was a mushrooming of retirement villages where the residents were routinely medicated at dinnertime. The assumption was that the elderly need some sort of help or support in the form of a pill just because they are getting older.

Other substances

Some people come to benzos via other substances – chemicals, medication or alcohol. For example they may have taken mind-altering drugs such as anti-depressants or major tranquillisers. If these produced anxiety or other unpleasant side-effects – as they often do – they were then treated with benzos. One woman was prescribed Valium to treat the headaches and nervous palpitations she developed from using chemicals to preserve plants. Alcoholics were routinely put on benzos to help them to dry out and kick their habit.

I had been drinking alcoholically for eight years. Finally I could stand it no longer and took an overdose of barbiturates and ended up in hospital for recovery. I was weaned off alcohol and put on Serepax, a fantastic new drug, 'good' for alcoholics especially, to calm their nerves.

Such people looked to benzos to help them recover from the harmful effects of other drugs, only to find that their saviour turned out to be a far more dangerous and persistent enemy.

Part I

....

Beating the
Benzo Sickness

Getting Addicted

Your life falls apart – you're not coping. You're put on benzos. The pills seem very helpful at first . . . they calm you down, give you the first good night's sleep you've had in months.

Time passes. Your life is back on track again. But somehow you are not feeling very well – not quite yourself. And you are still taking those pills which were prescribed to get you through the bad patch which was over long ago. It's very odd, really, because you're the sort of person who usually never remembers to take medication – you've never once finished a course of antibiotics. But somehow you still religiously take your dose of benzos – in fact you panic if you don't have one with you at all times.

No prizes for guessing the reason for this. You're addicted.

This is a chapter in the life story of hundreds of thousands of Australians. For the lucky ones the chapter lasts only a few months, but for many more it goes on and on for years. Why?

It was easier to understand in the 1960s and '70s before the addictive potential of benzos became widely known. In fact this information has been available since about 1970, but it was not generally accepted or publicised. Instead the drugs were touted as a miracle cure. Drug companies assured doctors they were safe and non-addictive, and doctors passed this information on to their grateful patients. At last there seemed to be a foolproof method for helping people through life crisis, anxiety and physical ailments associated with stress. In fact benzodiazepines were perceived as being so reliable that they were grouped with drugs prescribed for chronic life-threatening illnesses. People were often told that they had to stay on benzos for the rest of their days: 'They said I needed my Serepax like a diabetic needs insulin.' The wheels of addiction were oiled by the fact that benzos were easier to get than they are now. Once you were on board, time could be saved by leaving out consultations altogether. Getting your pills was a piece of cake – often all you had to do was ring up and a script would be left with the receptionist.

But these days we know much more about the addictive potential of benzos. Surely things have changed? Certainly prescription is now more restricted; a full history must be taken with every repeat. In 1988 the National Health and Medical Research Council issued guidelines to doctors advising that benzodiazepines should not be prescribed for periods of longer than four weeks. Even so, there are still 330,000* Australians taking benzos on a long-term basis.

* Andrea Mant *et al,* 'Benzodiazepine utilisation in Australia', *Australian Journal of Public Health 1993,* vol. 17, no. 4, pp. 345–49.

This is partly because there is still confusion and misunderstanding about what it really means to be addicted to benzos – and why it matters.

To begin with, the very word addiction is a problem in itself. Like 'criminal' or 'sadist', it has blaming, accusing implications already built in. It conjures up a mental picture of the world of street drugs; people injecting themselves with heroin in a seedy basement. Patients who are obediently taking small doses of a medicine prescribed by their doctor often resent having to identify them- selves in such a category. To try to overcome these connotations, the term 'dependence' is often used as a synonym. It sounds more polite, somehow much nicer, but it doesn't really further our understanding. What we need is a clear expla- nation of what benzo addiction really involves.

The Accidental Addict

Just as a car may be a Morris Minor or a Land Rover, addiction may mean many different things according to the substance in question. There are some factors that make benzos distinctive. For starters, most people who get hooked on sub- stances are well aware in advance of the risks involved. The heroin addict with his first fix, teenagers furtively lighting up behind the shelter sheds – they know about the possibility of addiction even though it may be only academic at that novice stage. In the past, people who became addicted to benzos rarely had that information, and they do not always have it now. In good faith they take a medicine given to them by their doctors. They are truly 'accidental addicts'.

Part of the attraction of most addictive substances, from heroin to chocolate, is to get a positive kick, a rush of enjoyment and delight. There is a pleasure principle involved, and addicts long to indulge that pleasure again and again. Even years after giving up, ex-smokers will still report a nostalgia, a longing for that first puff of smoke. Benzo addicts almost never experience a rush of pleasure when they take a pill, nor do they feel a craving for the drug itself. They take pills to try to avoid sickness.

> I recently gave up cigarettes, and the comparisons are interesting. Occasionally I still feel like a ciggy, whereas I never feel like the pills. In a way I'd like to go back on cigs if they weren't so bad for you, but there's no way I'd go back on those pills. There's no desire. I don't think I ever had any feeling of pleasure in taking a pill, but with the cigarettes it's like tasting an enjoyable food; you like doing it. You weren't really feeling unwell, it was more identified with pleasure than the relief of a symptom. Cigs are tricky because you feel you are giving up a pleasure, but overall they are easier to get off.

In fact, it is common for people who have come off benzos to feel revulsion and loathing for them, and a real fear that they might ever have to take them again.

Tolerance

Another feature of conventional addiction, or 'classic dependency', is that you have to steadily increase the dose to get the same effect. The alcoholic starts slipping an extra gin before lunch, then with morning tea and so on. This is called tolerance to the drug – you need more and more to get the same effect, and so you end up on a much larger dose.

Tolerance of this kind does occur with benzo dependency. There may be a feeling that the drug is wearing off, or not working as well as it did before. A person who started off on three Serepax a day may then find themselves taking an extra half a tablet, then a whole one – and so on. And there are some people who try to alleviate their symptoms by increasing to very large doses of benzos, shopping around to different doctors to get enough of the drug to stay well. These are the so-called 'abusers', who often feel guilty and humiliated by the extent of their addiction. Of course they are much loved by the drug companies because they provide such convenient scapegoats. People on very high doses were supposed to be the only ones who developed any problems at all with benzos. It was argued that they had only themselves to blame because of their weak 'addictive personalities'.

But such people are a minority. The majority of accidental addicts stay on the dose they were originally prescribed. They are dependent on just that dose; they don't ask for extra prescriptions, they just come back regularly to get them. Usually they have never been dependent on anything else, and they don't think to increase the dose because they are in the main very conscientious when following instructions.

Withdrawal symptoms

Because tolerance develops quickly and more of the drug is needed just to feel normal, those people who never increase their dose can, paradoxically, start to develop withdrawal symptoms on benzos sometimes as early as the first few weeks. This means that – unlike nicotine, for example – you can be in withdrawal while still actually taking the pills. Relief from symptoms can be obtained by taking more benzos – but only up to a certain point. Beyond that, it seems that the symptoms are there to stay no matter what dose you take. Even if you use benzos only two or three times a week, you can be affected eventually. Those who have been through this experience describe how, sooner or later, they hit the wall – that is, they get to a point where the symptoms dominate their lives. Many people use similar language to talk about how it felt: 'I seemed to reach a toxic level', 'My whole body felt toxic', 'It was as if I had been chemically poisoned.'

One woman sums it up like this: 'You are just as sick on the pills as you are off unless you are constantly increasing your dose. Even if you are constantly increasing, in the end you will be sick.' If this is not fully understood, both patients and doctors can easily fall into the trap of thinking that benzo addiction simply doesn't matter. If it is assumed that the pills are doing you good, then it is all right to be dependent. But if it is the pills that are actually causing symptoms of ill-health, then the picture changes dramatically.

I took Valium for over ten years. I was certain that it was the only thing that stood between me and a complete nervous breakdown. I'd known for ages that those tablets were addictive – I'd read various articles about it in newspapers and magazines. The message I got from them was that needing to take the tablets was wrong in itself, almost a bit of a sin. I couldn't relate to that because I saw them as medicine, not drugs. Surely it mattered what you were addicted to? I mean, would it be a bad thing to be hooked on lovely green salads? So whenever I saw those Valium-addict type articles I used to say to myself, 'So I'm addicted – who cares? Those pills are saving my life and I need them.' How wrong I was! Had I come off the drug before I got so ill I might have saved myself years of suffering. I was in a sort of daze for a lot of that time, but looking back now I can see that the state I was in was just getting worse and worse.

Something is Stalking Me

What is this illness and how does it reveal itself? Benzo sickness involves as many as seventy different symptoms affecting the body, mind and feelings. Some of these are: nausea, abdominal pain and discomfort, diarrhoea, vomiting, dizziness, flu-like symptoms, difficulty breathing, hormonal imbalances, incontinence, muscular pain, severe headaches, tremors, as well as agoraphobia, anxiety, panic attacks, depersonalisation, depression, fearfulness, insomnia and nightmares, lack of concentration and memory, mental confusion, rage and aggression, rapid mood changes and suicidal thoughts. The number and intensity of the symptoms varies from person to person, as does the time of onset. Symptoms may first appear a few short weeks after someone starts taking the pills. For others it is months, even years before they begin to feel sick. As the illness steals up and takes hold, people become puzzled and scared. They wonder what can be the matter with them. It seems that they are somehow getting worse, but they don't know why.

'I'm more anxious now than I was before'

Where benzos have been prescribed for anxiety, the relief people feel in those first few honeymoon weeks, when the pills start to work, is enormous. But when, after a while, they begin to feel anxious again they often panic, believing they have become exceptionally nervy. Back they go to their doctors and psychiatrists.

> I had anxiety, and at times felt so panicky that I had to go home from work. I went to two psychiatrists during this period and they tried to help, but I think what they were seeing was the effects of the benzos. They treated me with more pills. I thought I had become a very anxious person and they were telling me that as well. They said that maybe I would have to take benzos for the rest of my life. The doctors did not get it right at all.

It is important to note that it is not just those who are prescribed pills for anxiety who suffer. People given benzos for something else entirely, like period pain or muscle spasm, also develop strange anxiety symptoms that they never had before. Of course this frightens and baffles them. No one explains that it is most likely connected with their benzos.

Benzodiazepines are regularly prescribed for panic attacks, but people often find – after a brief spell where they have been free of them – that the attacks return. Often, the attacks are more frequent, more intense and last longer. People feel terrified but do not know why – one minute they are okay and the next moment they want to run or they become paralysed with fear.

> One day while I was on the pills, I was on the phone at work, perfectly routine. Suddenly, I felt faint and dizzy, peculiar, and I was sweating. I thought I was going to pass out. I had to get someone else to take the call. That was the first panic attack.

When this happens it is hard to know what is going on if you have never had or even heard of a panic attack.

> I experienced waves of panic. I can't say why. Once I just opened the door at work and someone was coming up the staircase – we didn't even bump into each other but it was a shock to see someone, and that induced a most terrible attack.

'My insomnia is so much worse'

One third of all benzo scripts are given for sleep problems. But it is now known that the hypnotic effects of benzos are lost after three to fourteen days of continuous use. After that, sleep in fact will often be disturbed. Only in retrospect do most people realise that the quality of sleep has been badly affected.

> The reason why I know the physical reaction to the benzos is pretty strong is because all of a sudden they stopped working. For some time

I'd have one quarter of a Mogadon and go to sleep within half an hour, wake up and feel fine. Then they stopped working. Sometimes I'd go to sleep, wake up, couldn't get back to sleep so I'd have another quarter. It took me four years to start upping the dose. I'd take the other quarter but it still wouldn't work, and I'd wake up feeling terrible – hung-over and groggy. Then I'd go to bed and I would just lie there in nothing like a sleep – so I'd take another quarter and lie there and still nothing would happen. I used to sleep a lot better than this before I even started taking benzos.

'I seem to be exhausted all the time'

Gradually, month by month, an all-pervading fatigue and weakness creeps over people. It is not the sort of healthy tiredness experienced after working for a day in the garden, but a wake-up-tired feeling, as if the life force has been drained away. Just getting up out of a chair can often seem an overwhelming effort.

I noticed during the last year on pills that I was completely drained of the energy I once had. It was quite common to spend almost a whole weekend in bed – I would get up, have a shower, make the bed and then lie down again for the rest of the day. I was weak and shaky and I could scarcely walk to the bus stop. My elderly aunts have much more energy than I had.

Agoraphobia

Like the other symptoms of benzo sickness, agoraphobia usually starts gradually, with little hints
here and there: an uneasy feeling in cinemas and
restaurants, and relief when you get home or back in
the car.

These sensations are mostly ignored and put
down to tiredness or just shelved and not thought
about. After all, everyone feels a bit strange from
time to time. Then people start to feel dizzy and
uncomfortable when they are shopping, a little
nervous in the supermarket, especially in the
queue at the register. But it is not until these
symptoms become more regular and more dis-
abling that they start to realise there is something
very wrong.

> I barely understood what the word agoraphobia
> meant before – I had a vague picture of an Ancient
> Greek standing in a huge market square, scream-
> ing with terror. But after about a year on Valium I
> started to get these strange wobbly out-of-control
> feelings whenever I was outside, walking or dri-
> ving. I read up on it and realised that I had agora-
> phobia. Eventually I found a support group, but I was
> too agoraphobic to get there. If only I had known
> that agoraphobia was caused by the pills I would
> have stopped taking them. I know now it is an
> early warning sign.

Driving ability is badly affected by these agoraphobic sensations. People who have driven in
busy traffic for years start to feel uneasy when

they have to drive in peak hour. They generally pass it off as tiredness and forget about it. Then, a few weeks or months later they have a panic attack at the traffic lights – they can barely make it across the intersection.

> I used to drive in the city all the time – I thought nothing of it. Then one day I felt a bit edgy and I was glad to get out, to get back to my office. A while later, I don't remember how many months, it happened again and then a few days later I was waiting at the railway gates for a train to pass and I had this overwhelming urge to drive into the gates, a sort of an agitation, like I couldn't sit there any longer. It petrified me.

'My brain used to work really well'

Rational decisions become more and more impossible as people slowly lose the ability to concentrate. Their minds can't stay on the job and their work suffers.

> A lot of my work involved talking to people, sorting out problems and things like that, but I was finding it difficult to see people and deal with them. I think that if I hadn't been drugged I would have insisted that I be given another job, but I was doped to the eyeballs and not able to sort things out. I was very confused – I wanted to get married and have a baby, go to university and go back to England, all at the same time!

A mental clouding seeps into people's minds.

Just doing daily tasks such as shopping becomes a burden – they can't think what to buy. They continue on, hardly aware of what is happening. Others, however, find they start to have trouble doing tasks which they have done competently for years. They can't focus on the job in hand; they begin to think they need a holiday or change of job.

> After eighteen months on Valium I found I couldn't concentrate properly – I couldn't do my work very well. Instead of helping me, the drugs worked against me. I couldn't get from A to B in a straight line because I couldn't see B – the pills were clouding my mind so much that I couldn't see ahead of me – I was beating around the bush. That almost cost me my job a few times.

Memory deteriorates, making it hard for people to deal with everyday life. They can't work out why they keep forgetting what has just been said to them and begin to fear the worst.

> I became really frightened when I realised that I was losing my memory – I was getting like my aunt who had senile dementia. I couldn't remember where I put things and even forgot my own telephone number at times. I was referred to a neurologist because I was sure I had a brain tumour.

'Somehow I've changed'

Personalities change. It happens so slowly that those who are close may sense that something is not quite right, but can't pin it down. They think that perhaps their companion is just worried or tired, and that it will all work out.

> I used to love a party, loved chatting to people – I liked it so much I used to talk to people when I was stuck in a queue, at the bank or post office. I was a fairly confident person, I just did things, I never thought about it. But after a while on the pills I couldn't talk to people at all – I felt weird, not myself. But I didn't tell anyone – I just plugged on hoping I would feel better, blaming the pressure of my job and family problems. I stopped wanting to go out – going out was a torment.

The trouble is, people do not recover while they are still taking benzos – they do not become their old selves. They get worse. Where they were placid and even tempered, they are now edgy and moody. They may stop doing many of the things they loved without even realising they are changing. And for some, this change in personality can be much more sinister. Huge mood swings can occur, with uncontrollable bursts of anger leading to violent acts which can contribute to child abuse and domestic violence.

> I would have these incredible mood swings and go off into these trances. I ill-treated my daughter until she was seven – I couldn't love her, I couldn't kiss her, and I couldn't stand my husband kissing me.

'I'm starting to feel so depressed all the time'
It is generally agreed now that long-term use of
benzodiazepines can cause depression – at times,
quite severe depression leading to suicide. Benzos
often make people who have had a history of
depression much worse.

> I was taking Valium each night to sleep. It is only
> when I look back that I realise that the sadness
> and misery I started to feel after many months was
> actually caused by the pills. I kept trying to find
> other things in my life which were making me
> depressed but I couldn't work it out – things were
> not that bad, just the ordinary ups and downs that
> happen in life.

Searching for Answers

More tests and chasing cures

Afflicted by so many bizarre symptoms, people think they have developed anything from a brain tumour to allergies. They keep going back to doctor after doctor, time and time again: 'I saw four psychiatrists, a naturopath and finally an occupational therapist.' Doctors themselves are uncertain about what is wrong. Unfortunately, the wrong diagnosis is made at times, with people being told they have an illness like arthritis, irritable bowel syndrome and even multiple sclerosis. So when sufferers consult doctors with a range of symptoms from chest pain to skin rashes, they are often sent for diagnostic tests. Hundreds of thousands of dollars are spent each year for tests.

I had X-rays for my back, all sorts of examinations, and two bouts of minor surgery for my urinary problem. I also had a colonoscopy and a barium enema for the bowel and that was negative. I thought I had heart trouble, an ulcer, organic nervous problems and I thought I was going mad. I was sent to a diagnostic clinic for a complete medical check for all these things. I also had a neurological examination. The results were negative, so I was referred to a psychiatrist.

When tests keep coming back negative and visits to psychiatric counsellors do not help, people look elsewhere to identify their symptoms. They read every magazine article they can find describing illnesses which may sound a little like what they are experiencing. They listen to friends who have found a new way of relieving stress and many seek advice from alternative therapists. They can end up going to a psychologist, a naturopath, a relaxation therapist, as well as asking the priest for advice – all in the same week.

> This illness has cost me a fortune. I think I have been to nearly every type of alternative doctor you could name – I've tried everything from acupuncture to hypnotherapy. I did yoga, meditation and drank herbs which smelled vile. I was desperate. I didn't know why I was feeling weird and ill – I couldn't get a handle on it at all. My life was busy but it had been much more difficult and stressful at other times, so why was I feeling like this?

'Am I *going crazy*?'

A psychiatric counsellor is the next cab off the rank when the various tests reveal no underlying physical illness. Some practitioners are unaware of the severity of the withdrawal syndrome and can advise people to stop taking their pills suddenly, which makes them extremely ill. Often they continue to treat their patients while these people are still taking benzos.

> I had constant headaches, anxiety, depression and nausea. The psychologist told me that I was like this because my mother was dominating me – all that garbage! – that I was a perfectionist and needed to learn to be more of a slob. But no mention of the pills – I would ask him about them but he didn't know about Serepax.

Once people develop benzo illness it is almost useless for them to seek help from a counsellor who is not experienced in benzo withdrawal because so many of the symptoms are chemically induced. It is very upsetting to receive conflicting advice about why they are feeling so weird.

> One psychiatrist told me I was suffering from depression and another told me I had nervous tension. They didn't know, and they blamed everything they could think of – my upbringing, my genetics, my job and my marriage.

Are more drugs the answer?

People are often prescribed anti-depressants when diagnostic tests reveal nothing of consequence. But benzodiazepines themselves are a depressant. People of cheerful temperament often look back and realise that they suffered from low-grade depression for most of the time they were on them.

People who are already depressed may become

despairing, even suicidal, on benzos. This then leads to a prescription for anti-depressants. These drugs are, in many cases, just treating the withdrawal symptoms – an extra chemical in the body to try to cure the adverse effects of the first one.

> I was depressed all the time while I took Ativan – that was why I took anti-depressants. I started taking them about a year after I was put on benzos. It was awful, just awful. I saw the psychiatrist every couple of months and we'd talk. At the end of the session he'd write me a script and I was always very relieved to get it.

When the effects of the pills are wearing off and the body and brain cry out for another benzo to get rid of the symptoms, the solution for some people is to turn to alcohol.

> I started to feel a bit better, but it didn't last . . . all the old feelings started to come back, along with more. Little did I know that I had become tolerant to the drugs and needed more, higher doses, as I was getting more and more withdrawal symptoms. By this time I had developed a two-fold problem. I discovered that drinking alcohol made me feel quite a lot better as it reduced my symptoms. Before taking the Valium I did not have a drinking problem, and now that I am no longer taking them, I do not have a drinking problem any more.

Anti-depressants are often added at this stage as people lose their confidence and become even more anxious. This is when a very dangerous

cocktail of cross-dependency can arise: benzodiazepines, anti-depressants and alcohol are a horrific combination. At worst it can kill. Some people
develop psychotic states for which major tranquillisers are often prescribed.

Another solution when the benzos are not
working as they used to is to up the dose. Some
people take extra pills as they feel they need
them. Others go back to their doctor who may
increase their dose, or put them on another type of
benzo.

> They were helpful at first but within a four-month
> period, I had increased the dose from one to two at
> night. I was waking up halfway through the night,
> and needing to take another one. So I just started
> taking the two before I went to sleep. By eighteen
> months I was taking three.

'I *thought it was me*'

It isn't easy to make the connection that the pills are
causing your symptoms or making them worse.
It's much more plausible to accept that it is just a
return of your original symptoms, particularly if
benzos were first prescribed for anxiety and
insomnia. Those who had their first script for
purely physical ailments are in a stronger position
here; they know they have never experienced
such weird things before, and so they can often
make the connection more quickly. The sad irony is
that most people blame themselves for their
symptoms – they think they are bringing it all on
themselves, that it is their own fault.

I didn't know what was causing all these symptoms, so I kept going to doctors. They kept saying I was anxious, and I was doing it to myself. I had read what tension does to you, and it does do similar things, so I thought, Hey, come on, it's in your hands to get well. Usually positive thinking helped, but I couldn't get out of this condition.

Making the Connection

Slowly, the information about benzo illness began to filter through. In the mid to late 1980s and early 1990s, people heard their symptoms being described on radio as 'the benzo withdrawal syndrome'. They saw TV programs explaining the dangers of prolonged use of benzodiazepines. Newspaper and magazine articles with personal stories described the severity and length of withdrawal. At long last there was someone else out there talking about their illness, and they began to think that perhaps it wasn't their fault after all.

'Thank God I was listening to the radio'

In 1987 a number of people in Victoria were listening to the same radio program about the problems associated with long-term use of benzodiazepines. They knew immediately that they had found the answer to what had been wrong with them all that time. One woman felt like a great weight had been lifted off her.

> I was home one morning, too weak to go to work and heard a woman on the radio talking about the symptoms caused by benzos. She was talking

about me – I knew that immediately. I was very excited and relieved – it was like a miraculous revelation but it also seemed obvious once I had the information. There was an 'of course' element to it. I was still a bit puzzled by the fact that I was taking such a small dose and was experiencing so many symptoms. I rang the agency named in the program and talked to a counsellor there who told me I had a very serious problem (I had been taking 5 mg of Valium per night for seven years). There was some initial hesitation – just delay rather than doubt – but I was absolutely resolved to get off them once I had the information about what had been making me so sick. It seemed like the most important task I had to perform.

Television programs, with people who had taken benzos participating, helped other people make the connection. One man happened to catch a television story about a Melbourne hospital which specialises in helping people come off benzodiazepines.

I quickly recognised the symptoms and realised that I had to get off my pills. The trouble is that most people I had spoken to before totally underplayed the withdrawal, as though it was just a bit of a headache for a few weeks. This was the first time I realised the seriousness of benzodiazepine addiction.

Many relatives and friends eventually realised how serious benzo illness could be when they read articles in magazines and newspapers highlighting people's struggles with benzo addiction. Community attitudes slowly began to change.

Health professionals recognise the problem

Articles about the addictive nature of benzodi-azepines were also appearing in medical journals. Patients began questioning doctors about the pills they were taking. Pharmacists too were concerned about the increasing use of benzos – very often explaining the risks involved in prolonged use and becoming equally worried when people abruptly stopped their pills.

> It was the chemist who told me that I couldn't throw them away like that. He had noticed that I hadn't had my script. He said that I had to ease off them. I said that I couldn't because they were gone and he was very concerned. I was determined not to take them again, and not to go back to the doctor. I was very busy that first day and raced around and did a lot of cooking, but after I had thrown them away I wished I hadn't.

A relieving doctor confronted one man with his addiction. His usual doctor used to comment that he was taking too many benzos, but he always shrugged it off thinking that he needed them.

> This relieving doctor was a psychiatrist. I gave him the usual sob story about being a nervy person and so on. He said, 'If you keep taking those tablets your nervous system is just going to turn to jelly. You won't be able to function – you'll get to the stage where the tablets will have no

effect on you.' I said, 'Are you sure?' and he said, 'Bloody oath I'm sure.' He frightened the life out of me.

I saw him at his private practice and he said that it wasn't the tablet that was helping me. I was feeding my addiction and that if I had any concerns or worries the pills were not doing anything to help them, it's just a chemical that's in your body and is doing all those things to you. He made sense. I thought, I haven't had any problems for years yet I was feeling this way and it didn't make sense.

What all these people had in common was hearing other people talk about the same symptoms they were experiencing, or having a health professional explain that the symptoms they were feeling were caused by the pills. They had not imagined their sickness and anxiety; there was a documented reason for their ill health. For most, their mind-set was changed, from being a non-coper to a person with a challenge. For some, the reaction was immediate, but for others it took a little longer to take up the responsibility for their recovery. But they no longer felt they were to blame.

Coming Off

Years after they have successfully overcome their addiction to benzos, people look back and remember how absolutely determined they were to get off their pills. Once they had enough information to put two and two together, nothing could stand in their way: 'That was it – I didn't want to put any more of that poison in my body.'

Many people try to come off and fail several times before they finally make it. Perhaps life takes a turn for the better – or maybe they get simply fed up with being controlled by a pill. Whatever the reason, they initially stop abruptly, usually with catastrophic results.

After I had been taking benzos for about six months I was feeling all right. I'd got over the problem with the relationship and I was doing better at work, so I thought I'd stop taking the tablets. No one explained to me how to stop taking them or what would happen if I did. One Friday night I decided to stop.

At that time I use to play in a band, and I remember vividly the Saturday night I nearly keeled over on the stage with dizziness and nausea. I had to hang on to the side of the stage to stand up. I thought there was something wrong with my nervous system – never did it occur to me that it was the withdrawal. I didn't tell the doctor – I'm not blaming him, he probably didn't know. I just kept going back to him and took benzos for years. I tried another couple of times to give them up but with the same result, only more pronounced, because as time goes by you need them more.

It is common for people to take benzos intermittently. Perhaps they have trouble sleeping or they feel nervous. Others are given a short course from time to time. When they stop taking them and feel well, they assume the pills are quite safe – or they are not the sort of person who will become addicted.

I had taken Valium, on and off, during the period of my divorce and simply stopped taking them without giving it a thought. Many years later I took benzos again for about eighteen months. I became really sick and I didn't know why. It was only luck that I saw an article about benzo addiction and realised what was wrong. It has taken years to get well this time. I now know that it can be quite safe to take benzos short-term, it is the long-term use which is dangerous.

Determination to come off pills is often mixed with fear. People are frightened of the pain they might suffer or of not being able to sleep. They don't quite know what to expect – everyone is different. They might be okay, but what if they're not and they can't make it?

> I was afraid to come off them. I was frightened of the panic attacks, I was frightened of the feelings I'd get – I wondered how far they would go. I knew if I took a tablet it would stop them. You were off them and you weren't going back on them, so there was the fear of the unknown in front of you. But I thought I could beat the damn things. And I did.

Once people are resolved to come off, there are many choices still to be made. What is the best method? Should they stop their pills right away or do it slowly? Is it necessary to go into hospital? What agencies and counsellors are available? Can they keep working? What is best for them?

Cold turkey

Many people feel a very powerful urge to just stop taking the pills, to get them out of their lives: 'I put my Valium into a plastic bag, then I buried it.' This impulse is understandable, but experience shows that people can become extremely ill if they come off benzos abruptly – especially if they have been taking them long-term. It can precipitate visual and auditory hallucinations as well as convulsions and acute psychotic states.

> I just stopped altogether. I thought it would be very unpleasant and it would last for a couple of weeks, then I'd start to get better. But of course it doesn't happen like that. I went back to the doctor because I was in a terrible state. He wanted to give

me another benzo but I wouldn't take it – I wanted to get off pills. I couldn't even speak properly, I couldn't sit down I was so agitated. I had trouble just putting my hand in my pocket to get out the medical card. Walking back out to the receptionist was awful because I was so dizzy, and the ground felt like it was moving. I was in such a bad state, I don't know how I got home. I don't think he should have sent me home like that.

Hospitals and agencies

Some people, for their own reasons, choose to go into hospital to come off their pills. Perhaps they have no one to look after them at home, or they may have been on a high dose for a long time and fear severe withdrawal.

In the early days, hospitalisation could be a very unpleasant experience. Very little was known about the special needs of people coming off benzos. Medication was often cut down far too quickly: 'I was off all my pills in about a week. I was dreadfully ill and really depressed.' What is good for other forms of addiction withdrawal programs is not necessarily good for people coming off benzos. For example, exercise is disastrous.

At the hospital they did aerobic exercise which I was completely unable to do. At the end of it I couldn't do anything stressful, and they laughed at me. I had always been good at sport, robust and well co-ordinated, and it was awful to be laughed at in this way. There were two or three others coming off benzos and they couldn't do the aerobics either. The people withdrawing from alcohol had no problems exercising after a few days.

These days most hospitals use a much slower withdrawal program involving at least a four-week stay. The patients are encouraged to take responsibility for their own recovery, and they have some say in their treatment program. People who have been on larger doses go home still taking their pills. They are monitored by a doctor, and they can attend support groups. If they are really scared or have no one to help them, they can go back into hospital to come off the last little bit. They can attend as out-patients for as long as they need to. These hospitals offer relaxation programs, meditation and counselling.

> I came off benzos in a drug-rehabilitation hospital. They taught us relaxation, how to rationalise things out; that the effect of benzos wasn't our fault (I had terrible guilt) and to take time out for ourselves. They told us about the withdrawal symptoms, that they would be an ongoing thing. They helped us learn how to manage them as best we could, one day at a time.

People who are not on large doses are able to come off benzos at home with the help of a well-informed and sympathetic doctor or an agency which specialises in benzo withdrawal. A good agency offers written information, one-to-one and telephone counselling, support groups and up-to-date information about what to expect when the benzos are stopped. And most importantly, people

are believed when they ring up and describe some of
their bizarre symptoms.

> I came off with the help of an agency. I was seeing a
> counsellor who monitored a very gradual reduc-
> tion of my small dose. The reduction took about
> two months. I used to ring up all the time – they
> were very patient, always reassuring and
> extremely helpful. If not for them, I might still be
> taking that poison.

The majority of people feel most comfortable
coming off benzos slowly, reducing their dose
over a period of months. In a few cases, if they
have been on very high doses, it can be years. For
those who are working, the reduction is best done
very slowly. It often enables them to bypass the
extremely severe symptoms that make work
impossible. They can still have a prolonged withdrawal, with some severe symptoms, but they are
more able to manage them.

> I came off benzos very, very slowly over a period of
> one and a half years. Having a job, it would have
> been difficult or even impossible to have done it
> any faster. I was determined to keep my job – I
> needed it financially. There wasn't a set procedure
> like cutting down every three months. I cut down
> the pills and then I waited until I had stabilised and
> felt a bit better and was confident that I could make
> another cut. If I felt I wasn't up to reducing, I wouldn't.

People manage best if they are well informed
and choose a method they feel comfortable with.

Once they have made the decision to stop, their withdrawal should suit their needs. Some can cope with a quick withdrawal and manage to come off their pills quite fast, especially if they are on a low dose. But if they try a fast withdrawal and it doesn't suit them, they can drop back to a slower reduction.

Coming off long-term use of benzos has often been described as the toughest thing people have ever done: 'It was hell. The agency gave me a list of symptoms and I seemed to get nearly every one of the damn things, at one time or another.'

A full description of the withdrawal experience and symptoms can be found in A–Z of Symptoms, page 157.

Recovery – How Long?

> Two weeks after I came off, I was resting in the lounge when my mother came in and said, 'What's the matter with you? You've been off those tablets for a fortnight now, you should be all right.'

But he wasn't all right. This man was still very ill, and he did not know how long it would be until he recovered. He was facing the great puzzle of benzodiazepine withdrawal: how long will it last? Unfortunately there's only one accurate answer – the most frustrating answer of all. It depends entirely on the individual – everyone is different.

Benzodiazepine withdrawal isn't like flu or chickenpox – it has no familiar well-documented patterns. It is one of the most erratic and unpredictable of all human ailments. Some people who are badly affected while still taking the pills report feeling much better and having few further problems as soon as they stop. Some suffer only mild withdrawal symptoms for a short while before complete recovery. But others, looking back on their withdrawal journey, report that many symptoms continued to plague them for months, even years.

I've been off my pills for years now. I'm very much better than I was, but I'm certainly not recovered. I've made an enormous amount of progress though. I do have symptoms that linger on, but I've got rid of a lot of things. The first year and a half I really wasn't functioning at all. Particularly in the first year I was very, very sick. It's nothing like that these days, but I still don't feel well. I don't dwell on it, it's something I have learnt to live with.

Even at six years off pills, I'm not completely better, but I still keep improving. I'd rate myself about six out of 10. I'm still learning to cope with life on a daily basis without pills. In the past my way of coping was to take a pill. Physically I've just about recovered; emotionally I think I've got a fair way to go. I lead a pretty hectic lifestyle and handle it pretty well. At three years off I lacked confidence on a lot of days, lacked motivation, often felt tired and physically sick. Whatever I wanted to do looked and felt absolutely enormous. I'd wake up in the morning and know I had to wash and iron but would just want to stay in bed all day. Now I leap out of bed raring to go for the day. I haven't had that constant sense of being in withdrawal that you live with all the time for about three years now.

When it was first recognised that benzos caused dependence and a withdrawal syndrome, the usual time given for recovery was between two to four weeks. Not pleasant, but not a very large chunk out of the average human life. There was no precedent for a much longer drug withdrawal period; most studies for alcohol, nicotine or opiate addiction did not follow up subjects for much longer than a month.

However, evidence began to pile up from people coming off benzos who were experiencing symptoms for very much longer than four weeks. Other ways of estimating the length of the process were invented. One of these was that withdrawal would last one month for every year that you had taken the pills. But when sufferers did their arithmetic, they found that they had passed the due date and were still experiencing symptoms. It was becoming obvious that there was not much point in trying to calculate the exact time recovery takes; in fact it can be actively unhelpful as it leads to disappointment and discouragement when the prediction turns out to be inaccurate.

It is possible for benzo withdrawal symptoms to last two years and more – indeed people can still be affected three, four, five years down the track. The reason for this is still not clear. One theory holds that the chemical is stored in fatty tissues, and is released only very gradually as the body detoxifies. It has also been suggested that the natural chemical processes of the brain take a long time to begin to function properly again once benzos are stopped. But until adequate research is done, this is only speculation. What we do know from observation is that withdrawal symptoms come in little clusters or bursts. They are sometimes just as acute as they were in the beginning, but they usually get milder and less frequent as recovery progresses.

It's six years since I took that last quarter of Valium and threw the rest in the garbage. At that time I was expecting to be completely well within a few months. I wasn't. For the first year I was too sick to do much but lie around at home. Then I was able to work for a couple of days a week, and from that time on I got slowly, slowly better. About that time I stopped raging against it and asking why me; I just tried to accept it quietly. Sometimes I'd get a really dreadful bout of symptoms, sometimes just touches of this and that, fatigue, social phobia, funny bowels. I was used to them by that time – they seemed like horrible old relatives who I put up with. Even now I can get the odd benzo thing – and I know my tolerance to stress is less than it was. But I also know now it will go on improving, and I don't let it interfere with my life.

Is it better not to know?

The possibility of a prolonged withdrawal period raises an urgent question for health workers in this field, and for people who have recovered and are helping others who have just come off their drugs. Naturally everyone wants to return to normal and get on with their lives as quickly as possible. So how much should they be told about the possibility that recovery may not be as quick as is hoped? Isn't it likely that those who are still on their pills simply refuse to come off if they know recovery could take so long? Mightn't people who are off their pills become discouraged, throw in the towel and go back on their pills? Is it better for them not to know that, in some cases, withdrawal can last for months or even years?

Ultimately it is better to be honest, even if it means that some individuals stay on their pills. In every area of medicine it is now recognised that people have the right to be fully informed about all matters affecting their health. Those in benzodiazepine withdrawal, too, have the right to be treated like competent adults instead of children in need of protection. As well as these ethical considerations, there is the purely practical danger of withholding information about the possible length of recovery. Unless people are warned that they might be unwell for some time, they cannot plan their lives effectively. For example one man, believing that he would be recovered within weeks, left his family business and set up on his own in the building trade. The venture failed because he was far too ill to manage. Had he known, he would never have made such a dramatic life-change at that time.

If they are not fully aware of how long the withdrawal might last, people can and do conclude that the symptoms they are experiencing are once more 'just them'. They struggle through nine months or so of withdrawal, but they don't seem to be getting very much better. It is all too easy to fall back into thinking that they are incurables and might as well resign themselves to a lifetime of non-coping. So they go back on the pills, falling yet again for the old line, 'it is all your own fault'. But if the symptoms are due not to their 'neurotic personalities' but to detoxifying from a chemical, then people can have faith that withdrawal will pass in time, and that they will be restored to normal health.

Lives Turned Upside Down

> Withdrawal disrupted my life in every way –
> disrupted my relationships, disrupted my friend-
> ship system, disrupted my work, disrupted my
> income.

Family and friends

There are many experiences in prolonged benzo
illness that damage people's ability to relate to
others, even those they love best. It is hard to be a
warm, considerate companion if you are suffering
from high anxiety, depersonalisation, mental confusion, claustrophobia or any of the other sev-
enty-odd withdrawal symptoms in random
combination. It becomes an endurance test for
everyone concerned. Family members are often
puzzled and distressed. The person they loved –
the wife they shared everything with, the mother
who was so much fun, the dependable husband – is
gone.

Instead there is a stranger who does not want
to do things with the family, who avoids friends
and relatives, who seems to be sick and anxious
almost all the time. The erratic nature of the

illness, and the fact that on some days people are apparently perfectly well, makes it even more confusing. Such things can be borne for a short time, but over a longer period they lead to disappointment, anger on both sides, and in some cases even the breakdown of family relationships.

It's only the people who love me who have stuck by me, and they've found it very difficult, because I'm always crying or I'm whingeing and whining about how sick I feel. How many years can you put up with that? My daughter-in-law came in after work, and she said to me in an accusing tone, 'So you've got that headache back again? I thought that had gone.' She loves me, but she is sick of seeing me with a headache. My family don't want to know about my illness. They want the lovely capable gran who will listen to their troubles.

My eldest virtually did everything. She was forced to grow up a lot more quickly than she would have done because Mum wouldn't move out of the house. I don't know how many times I said, yes, we'll go to the park, we'll do this or that. I promised them, all full of good intentions, because I really wanted to, but I couldn't. They get so disappointed, they don't understand. The first four years of my younger daughter's life were a total wipeout because of those stupid tablets, and you don't get that time back.

My wife and kids had to put up with me while I was slowly getting rattier and rattier. Your close family get to the stage where they think you aren't being truthful. They can't understand why after such a length of time you don't want to do anything. My family had the attitude that if I had enough gumption I'd pull myself together and try to do something. I ended up being very angry about their attitude.

Friendships suffer perhaps even more than family relationships during a long benzo recovery. You must make plans and organise outings to see your friends – you have to make a deliberate effort, and that is just what people in benzo withdrawal cannot do. They fear the commitment involved in a social engagement because they can't predict what symptoms they will have on that particular day. Instead they tend to avoid people – and if you avoid people for long enough they'll start to avoid you too. This causes anguish for benzo sufferers who don't want to alienate friends but feel helpless to prevent it.

I wanted desperately for people to come round and knock on my door and help me, but on the other hand I couldn't give anything to anyone. It was hard enough reserving enough strength for myself.

I didn't care about my friends any more, I was too introverted and focused on my own problems to notice anyone else. I avoided people. I knew I'd have to socialise if they came – they'd want me to go somewhere or do something. I didn't want to do it, and I didn't want to make an excuse about why I didn't want to do it. So I figured it was a lot better if they just left me alone. And in the end they did leave me alone. I must have dropped enough hints that I didn't want to do anything – though it was really a scream for help. But people don't necessarily see what you want them to see.

It affected my relationships with most people because I didn't feel like going round to explain why I was moody and uncommunicative. So I wouldn't communicate with people – I would keep out of their way. If I saw someone coming I would go round a corner – I've lost quite a few friends that way because they thought I was avoiding them.

But it is not just avoidance which damages relationships with others. People in withdrawal can often behave very badly, in a way which is quite out of character. One of the many paradoxical effects of benzos is disinhibition, which means that the inner censors which normally stop you from doing and saying hurtful things are removed. This can lead to angry outbursts and spiteful attacks destructive to harmony with both family and friends.

I behaved horribly to my boyfriend, and I really regret it now. Just out of the blue I would say vicious insulting things which undermined his confidence. Looking back now I can't believe I said those things to another human being, let alone someone I loved. I never had that tendency before. In the end it poisoned the relationship. He never really forgave me, and I don't blame him. I tried to explain my behaviour as being part of my withdrawal from Valium, but he couldn't stomach that – and why should he? He once said to me that he wished he had something he could use to account for his bad behaviour. I don't blame him for that reaction either. Although I knew it was true about the withdrawal effects, I still felt like I was trying to make cheap excuses.

I don't know how much it had to do with my marriage break-up. I was telling my husband things I'd never told him, and our marriage had been based on my not saying certain things. I've always been extremely alert to people's needs, wants and feelings, and tried to look after them. In withdrawal I felt I could still see what was upsetting people but I didn't seem to want to get involved with them. There was a clumsiness: saying the wrong thing, not saying things you knew you should say. Everything was badly timed or inappropriate, excessive or too little.

To tell or not to tell?

A dilemma which crops up sooner or later for everyone who is having a hard time in benzo recovery is just how much you should talk about it. Is it a good idea to be frank with your family, friends and colleagues about what is happening to you?

One of the main problems with telling people that you are sick because of prolonged benzodiazepine withdrawal is that it's hard to get them to understand or to take it seriously. The syndrome is not widely known or recognised. It does not have the status of a legitimate illness. Rather it is in the vague malingerers' basket along with mysterious complaints such as chronic fatigue syndrome. Most of the publicity about benzos has concentrated on the 'Valium addict – pills from hell' side of things because it is sensational in a way that a long illness is not. Credibility is not helped by the fact that sufferers may look perfectly well even when they are enduring crippling anxiety or depersonalisation. If they try to talk about it, they run the risk of being met with irritation and disbelief – and nobody likes to be labelled a whinger.

Whether or not people tell is once again a completely individual decision according to temperament and circumstances. Once again there's a range of approaches, from those who are completely frank with family, friends, boss and colleagues to those who tell no one. Some have an almost missionary zeal about being honest. They tell because they feel they have nothing to blame themselves for – they need not be embarrassed about becoming an accidental addict. Some decide not to tell because they are sure that no one will believe them and that no one is interested anyway. Others are ashamed of the stigma attached to their addiction, and fear that it will lead to rejection and humiliation.

Responses range from care and support to the annoyance and scepticism of the pull-up-your-socks-it's-all-in-your-mind brigade. But even those whose nearest and dearest are very supportive at first find the longer haul wearing. They find it hard to believe that symptoms could still persist after a year.

You have to give some explanation, so why not be truthful? I got to the stage where I didn't care what people thought – I told them the truth, that I'd got addicted to a drug through no fault of my own, and that I was going through withdrawal symptoms. What else is there to say? I hated admitting that I needed drugs for a nervous condition, but you've just got to be honest and be yourself.

I told people but didn't make much of it. They were supportive. I told one close friend about it and gave her literature to read. I told her that if I said I'd go to a certain show with her it depended on how I felt that day, and I wasn't going to push myself. She accepted that in the early days, but I don't think she'd accept it now – she'd think I wasn't making enough effort.

To work or not to work?

One of the most urgent questions to be resolved if recovery might take a while is whether or not it is possible to keep on working. Many people do stick with their jobs throughout withdrawal, often at great cost to their health and sanity. Keeping up with the demands of the workplace can be very stressful, and of course the degree of stress varies with the type of job. Work which requires a high level of social interaction or public performance, concentration and memory, or physical effort is particularly taxing. Asked to imagine the ideal job for a person in withdrawal, many people come up with the picture of themselves quietly stamping books in some remote library.

Those who do continue to work usually find that it takes every last bit of energy they have for that day. When they come home they can't do anything but collapse.

> I kept a full-time job all through. I was not always very productive, but I kept the job going. I was having trouble working. I'd sit at the desk, stay away from people, not join in with what was going on. I'd be very vague. I certainly used a lot of sick-leave just by taking a day here and there. Once I had done my job I had nothing left over, that was about all I could cope with.

But although it is an exhausting struggle, people who are able to stick with their jobs generally agree that in the long run it was good for them. The social contacts, the discipline, and the sense of self-esteem which they gained from their efforts to overcome their disability were all rated very worthwhile.

> I stayed working and it makes you do things. You cannot feel sorry for yourself when you work. I was very honest with people at work when I couldn't do things. I told the people at work I was with-drawing from pills and their reaction was very different. One person admired me because I was trying and coming to work when I was so ill. I thought, yes, she is right, I drag myself out of bed in the morning, drive myself to work half-terrified of the traffic – work all day feeling nervous and ill. She is right – I should be proud of myself.

The way in which benzo withdrawal can disrupt careers, the difficulties which can arise, and the courage needed to face them, can be seen in one man's work history.

When I first started taking the pills I left a job that was highly paid – I was head-hunted by another company. But I spent most of the time trying not to be ill. I had to go to a lot of business lunches, and I became paranoid about that, I used to fear it. Inevitably people drank, and I'd have a glass of wine too, and it would make me feel extremely ill. I asked the doctor and the chemist and they said one or two glasses were okay. I didn't realise then that even a small amount could make you feel very unpleasant.

My difficulties were very noticeable – I was performing at about ten per cent of my capacity with odd flashes of genius which bridged the gap. Eventually it was obvious that I would have to leave. After that I got a job handling mail. I went from a senior executive position to this menial job. I was so weak by then that I could hardly lift the postbag. It was just at that time that I stopped taking the pills. I'd be sitting there trying to open envelopes, and suddenly this awful nausea would overwhelm me. I left that job still feeling ill and got a job at another company at a level somewhat below what I was accustomed to. I felt ill throughout that time – the agoraphobia was debilitating. The train journeys to work were hell.

After thirteen months I resigned, and then there was a long period where I was unemployed. Now I have a job again – not a senior position, but it does have some creativity involved, and I am coping most of the time. I could not do a senior job yet.

It was easy to become paranoid because of the frequent judgement that you were not ill. This was completely unfair. I was in considerable pain, but those around me thought I was all right and that I could do things if I wanted to. I feel frustrated and angry that I have been made to lead a life of poverty by these pills when I have been offered two or three top-line jobs which pay very well. I have had to knock them back because I could not cope with them.

Some of those unlucky enough to suffer bad withdrawal find that they cannot work at all, particularly if they are in jobs which are intellectually or physically demanding. They have no choice – they are simply not well enough. Others make a conscious decision that recovery is their most important goal, and that complete rest will help them to achieve that.

Another cause of hardship is the financial loss which is bound to be incurred if you have to stop working. Some people suffer the humiliation of being the family drone, having to be supported by those they used to support. Others live on their savings, or on sickness benefits. This can add up to a very large amount of savings, salary or investments lost.

In the end I wasn't earning any money, so I was a real millstone. My wife has worked round the clock to support us.

There was no way I could have worked in that first year, so I took leave without pay. I was too sick to even think about how to get on sickness benefits. Luckily I had some family money which I'd inherited, and it was just enough to live on until I could work again. Still I've blown all that money which I'd otherwise have invested as well as all the salary. It's a huge loss, tens of thousands of dollars.

Negatives and Positives

Withdrawal was the hardest thing I've ever done in my life, but also the most worthwhile.

This is the overwhelming feeling of most people when they successfully come off benzos. It is a tough process to go through: the fear, the weird feelings, the illness and pain, the alienation and the loss of income. But all these things are for a purpose – to be in control of their lives once again.

So hard to do

Nearly everyone who endures a severe and protracted withdrawal feels the same way: 'I think if you can go through all this, and survive, there's not much else that's going to worry you.' It is often very difficult to get through each day, let alone stay optimistic.

When I'm having a terribly bad day, I think that if I had known what I had to go through I probably might not have done it. Even six months ago I might have said no. I was fairly sick on the pills but I became a lot worse after I stopped taking them, so only time will tell whether it was worth it for me as far as symptoms are concerned.

'I'm not crazy after all'

Most of the anxiety and weird thoughts that have plagued people disappear in time. This is the most rewarding aspect of giving up benzos – the realisation that you are a sane, sensible, normally functioning individual.

It has been very difficult to get off the pills – it has taken me five years. There have been times when I have wondered whether it has been worth it, I was so ill. But when I think back, of course it has been worth it. I had no idea that the journey would be so hard. Psychologically I am much better – to be addicted to benzos is awful. I was also told I had become an anxious person. Now, knowing that it is not me, that it is the benzos which make you anxious and sick, is a relief.

'I can feel again'

The gradual return of emotions can be difficult as well as exhilarating. People affected by benzos tend to have their feelings numbed and flattened out – they avoid issues and go with the flow. In withdrawal, they must undergo a whole new learning process to deal with their emotions and other people's feelings.

I do think I am painting better because I am more able to show my feelings. I play the organ at the church, and I get feeling into my playing better. I am not so frightened of showing emotion now, either. I had some counselling and I learnt a lot about myself; I have access to a greater range of feelings now. I was always a little scared of handling emotions until I went through this, but you go right to the bottom, the depths, so now I know I can cope with emotion. I have learnt that it is best not to avoid pain; the pain of death, or the pain of growing old – it is best to face it. I find it helps to express it through painting, so that is what I do.

'I question things more now'

People who have been made ill by prescribed medication learn that it is important to take the responsibility for their body and mind very seriously. They become careful about what medication they take as well as what they eat and drink. They are much more demanding when they visit a doctor or therapist of any kind, and more confident about asking for information and discussing treatment.

I'd wash the feet and drink the water of all the people who got me off these pills. When I think of how I might have ended up if I had kept taking them . . . I believe what the doctor said to me, that if I'd kept on taking benzos my nervous system would turn to jelly. I was having to take so many to have the tranquillising effect that they stupefied my brain.

This experience has taught me a lot about the human body and mind and I am a lot more cautious about accepting medication. I think that you can get through a lot of things with the right help rather than taking medication – help from professional as well as lay people.

A *second chance*

If people have been on benzos for a long time they may need to go back to that point in their lives when they started to take the pills to see if that problem still exists for them. If it was a life crisis, like a broken relationship or working two jobs, then it has probably passed long ago. If it is an ongoing problem like chronic anxiety then they may still have to do some work on it. People who have been on the pills a long time have often become very passive, and have lost the ability to negotiate and take their part in a discussion. They may now wish to re-evaluate their lives, and learn new skills to deal with stress.

Withdrawal was well and truly worth it because I have a lot better lifestyle now than I had when I was on benzos. I had to learn certain lifestyle skills to get off the pills and one of those skills was learning to say no to people and not try to please all the time. I put time aside now for relaxing activities and fitness. I do relaxation every day – morning and night – and meditate. I feel I understand myself much better now and I make sure I don't take on too much.

More understanding now

Because people are going through such a long and often bizarre illness, they find they can relate to others in the community who are sick or disadvantaged. And although the experience is horrific at times, they feel they have grown spiritually and very often support others who are just starting to come off their pills.

I am very, very glad I have stopped taking benzos. I've become far more philosophically and spiritually aware than I was before. Most people think that their number is up when they are coming off pills because the experience is so bad. It is a day-to-day survival (minute to minute sometimes) and you think that you can die at any time. You begin to rationalise a lot of things in life – you come out of the experience at the other end a different person. You understand other people more. The fact that other people do not understand what you are going through – the rejection you suffer from family and friends because they do not believe you or cannot cope with you – makes you more aware of the suffering of others. You do become more tolerant.

I now realise that you are alone out there unless you find people who have similar problems. So it is feeling alone, being in so much pain and the total rejection of most of society that helps you to understand how others, who have experienced difficulties in their lives, need more understanding. It has made me think more deeply about everything.

Part II

....

Accidental Addicts:
Their Stories

BRUCE
A soccer player knocked out

Bruce is in his early fifties. He is divorced and has four children. He took Valium for thirteen years, from 1973 to 1986. It was first prescribed because of a combination of factors: overwork, drinking, and the traumatic loss of two members of his family. For many years he drank while using pills, and his story shows what a deadly combination benzos and alcohol can be.

Even at five years off the pills, Bruce still has some withdrawal symptoms, and he is sure that Valium affected his personality. Once an outgoing gregarious Aussie bloke, he now lacks the self-confidence, motivation and social skills he had before.

I never thought much about health before my experience with Valium. Health was something you just had.

I used to play soccer a lot – up to four games a weekend. I was always an uptight sort of person though. Before a soccer match I would vomit and dry-retch even though I was captain of the side. The referees would say, 'This bloke's too sick to go on', until they got used to me, but once the game started I wouldn't worry, I'd just smack the first bloke beside me under the ear and I'd be into it, whereas the other blokes would take twenty minutes to warm up. Same with meetings. I'd shake and I'd go to the toilet but as soon as the meeting started I'd be right. I was always edgy.

In 1973, when I was thirty, my mother died, and then my brother was killed in a car accident after the funeral. There was a hitchhiker in his car, going back home after the funeral who was killed instantly, but they thought he was my brother because they had swapped places in Albury. I went to identify the dead body and got my hopes up thinking maybe it was the wrong car. In fact my brother lasted for about ten days in the Albury Hospital. In those days hospitals couldn't turn off the life-support systems – if they did they could be charged. The doctors said to me, 'If it's going to be done you have to do it.' So I turned it off. He lasted maybe another forty-eight hours. I have often thought maybe I killed him.

At that time I was working very hard. I was married with four children. I took a second job working nights in a pub on top of my day job as a personnel officer. The day job was stressful because a lot of people were being made redundant about that time. Also I was involved in a program to try to help the younger members of staff who were having problems with alcohol and drugs. I was very tired, so I went to the doctor. He prescribed Valium, and that's how it all started.

To be honest I was dependent on grog too, very much so. I was a bender drinker. Working at pubs you can finish at 11 pm – there's unlimited grog so you just stay there. The doctor knew I was drinking – that was part of the reason he gave me the tablets; he wanted to calm me down so I wouldn't drink.

I guess I started taking them and that was that; it became a habit, and I couldn't do without them. If I didn't take them I found I couldn't do my second job. I'd take two in the morning, two at lunchtime and two at night. I didn't increase the dosage at all at first – in fact I kept trying to reduce it, down to one in the morning then half and one, but every time I'd get the shakes and I'd increase it again. They kept telling me, you can't go off them. I'd go back and say I didn't like taking tablets, and they'd say, you're under too much stress, you just can't come off them. The doctor said I needed them like someone who has high blood-pressure needs their medication.

When I woke up in the morning I couldn't let my wife see me. I'd go and dry-retch in the toilet until I'd had that tablet, until it had got into my system. It got to the point where I'd get up an hour earlier than her just so I could take the tablet and stop the shakes. I'd go to bed before her so she wouldn't see me shaking. It buggered up my sex life. I withdrew into myself because of these night sweats and shakes, and my wife thought I'd gone off her.

While I was taking pills and drinking I used to have memory blackouts. This happened every couple of months. I had no recollection of where I'd been or what I'd done. One time I came to in Hobart and didn't know how I'd got there. By that stage I'd changed jobs – I was selling insurance. I wouldn't have any recollection of doing an insurance appointment until I was going through my papers at

the end of the week. I used to find insurance pro-
posals that I didn't remember writing.

When I got into trouble with the grog, most
times I was taking the Valium. I gave up drink
totally in 1979 for about three and a half years. I
thought it would improve my marriage but it
didn't.

I hated taking the tablets – it made me feel
morally weak. I got to the point where I would lie,
cancel appointments, say the car had broken
down and so on just to avoid taking an extra
tablet. I knew I was dependent on both grog and
pills – I couldn't go to a party without a drink or two.
But I could stop drinking and I'd be fine; I didn't
have the sweats or the shakes. I never had them
even when I was drinking really heavily. I could go
for weeks, months, without a drink.

With Valium it was different – I'd get the shakes if
I stopped. I think I was addicted from the first time I
took them. It wasn't a craving, it was a chemical
thing. I took pills just to function. Originally when I
went to a party with my wife she'd hang onto my
hand, but towards the end of my time on the pills I'd
hang on to her arm and shuffle like a little baby,
until I took a tablet.

In 1979 I rolled my car. My wife virtually said,
'I'm wiping you.' I put myself into a private detox
hospital to come off pills and grog. I was that
scared I was drunk as a skunk when I walked in
there. No medication – they cut it all out completely. I was going up the wall – I wouldn't let my
wife and kids come in. After ten days I just walked
out of there. On the way home a young kid tried to
commit suicide off the train. About four of us

grabbed him. I thought, God, that could have been me. No way! I lied to my wife; I told her I was okay without the Valium, but I went back to the doctor and just started with them again.

If one doctor wouldn't give it to me I'd go to another one. No doctor ever questioned it. I'd ask for a prescription with two repeats dated the next month, so I wouldn't have to go back again. A lot of doctors would do that. It got to the point where I was actually taking a lot more than I should have: approximately eight Valium per day. I thought that taking this many was the price of staying off grog.

That went on through the '80s and I finally got the dose down to half a tablet in the morning and quarter at lunchtime and at night. I knew I was going to have the shakes but I thought, okay, I'm just going to have to suffer. The boss thought I was drinking too much but I wasn't drinking at all. That went on till about 1985.

That year my wife and I went overseas for six weeks. I didn't want to go there with the shakes, so I took the tablets over with me. My wife discovered them when she was going through my bag to get the passports out. That was not a very happy trip. When we came back she just nagged me into giving it up.

I came off cold turkey. I wouldn't do it again. In March 1986 I took some leave and sat on my hands at home. I told the doctor what I was going to do and he said, 'You can't do it, you'll go mad and you'll finish up inside.' I said, 'well, I've got to do it for my own sake.' So I went through the cold sweats and being sick and not being able to get off the toilet, not eating . . . I wasn't going to go back into the hospital again because I felt that was hiding. I've always done things the hard way.

Right now I'm going through the worst period in my life, but there's no way I'd ever go back to the Valium. I'd cut my wrists rather than go back on them. Coming off was so horrific.

When I first came off I couldn't talk to people – I would break down. I thought I was going mad. People would ask me if I was drunk. And I'm still very anti-social. Before pills I would talk to any-body. Now it's usually okay after the first hour or so, but before then I think, ugh, what if someone talks to me. At the soccer last week some bloke sat beside me and I had to move – there was nothing wrong with him. I went back and said, 'I'm sorry, mate, it wasn't you.' There was quite a big crowd there and I deliberately sat at the end of the row. Now when I go to my son's matches I stand by myself. I used to stand with the other fathers.

I'll come home with the intention of going to the movies, but nine times out of ten I'll cancel it because I've come in and I'm safe here. I don't even go to people's places for dinner. Someone will knock on the door and I won't answer it. If people do come to the door I pick up my car keys and say, 'Oh, I'm just going out' – even to my daughter. Your friends can only take so much of you not ringing them back or not answering the door when they know you're here. I've had them belting and kicking the door. While they do that I'll just walk out and quietly go down the lane.

I don't want close relationships like I used to have with mates or my wife – well, I'd love to have them back but at the moment I can't interact with them.

I don't have much self-confidence. I have confidence that I can achieve, but not the way my employers want me to. They want me to do a public speaking course; I know I can't. I'm always scared I'm going to fall back on the Valium if I push myself too hard.

When I go to the library I'm too scared to tell them that I don't know how to work the catalogue computer, so I just go round the shelves and grab some books.

I go shopping just so I'm out of the house. I'm walking up the street, but I'm walking in the gutter so that people are away from me. There are some shops I can't go into yet because I've got to ask someone to serve me. For example there's a towel and doona shop nearby, and if it's not out the front where I can just walk in, pick it up and give them the money . . . I've been trying for two years to go in and ask for certain towels and certain doona covers, and I can't. I just cannot do it. They're all women there, and very few blokes come into those kind of shops. Yet before I could go into a bra shop and pick out a bra and a nightie – it wouldn't have worried me. I'd go in and ask for anything in a chemist's shop without being at all worried.

Nowadays even in a menswear shop if I can't see what I want before he asks me, I'm out of that shop. I go to a seconds shoe shop where no one serves me – I just pay the money and leave.

Before when I went to a soccer match I was really into it. If anyone disagreed with me I'd tell them where to go – not that I liked fighting, but I was so into it. These days I go to a match and I've got to be away from people, I don't want any aggro and I'll even shut up at a match, not even barrack in case I escalate someone else. I'm not scared of them, but I feel I don't need that aggro.

I'm tired all the time now. Some days I'll just sit here and do nothing. I'll even ring my son – I'm pretty close to my youngest son – and say I can't come to football, I have to work. I'll do that because I feel so lethargic I just don't want to go out. It's a way of not confronting life. I was never like this before I was on Valium. I could always face life. I think I'm trying not to pressurise myself too much.

When I wake up I feel tired. In my younger days I used to love the mornings. Even now I'll get up early because I'm not sleeping. The shaking in the morning may be because I force myself to do things. It wears off. I'm up and then I'm off, and even though I might have the shakes I've just got to do that appointment. Usually my first appointment in the morning is the one I botch up.

I look at everything now on a day-to-day basis: if I can get through the day that's all I worry about. I don't make any plans for the future. Basically I make plans for my kids' future but not for mine. So I really don't give it a lot of thought. I just get up because I have to get up. I don't feel great. I don't even feel great on the weekends, whereas I used to live for the weekends, I used to love the weekends. I don't feel any burning desire to do things.

What I try to do is not place myself under too much pressure. It's the wrong way to be but I'll try to avoid it. My job in a sense is the most pressurised job I've ever had, so I can't avoid every pressure, but I'll try to avoid a lot of it if I can. Because I never want to put myself at risk of taking Valium again.

I've been off pills for five years – but no way am I now completely recovered. I was very outgoing, I was very happy – apparently I give that same impression now, but I'm not. To be honest I didn't start maturing as a person until I came off the tablets, and now I'm maturing more in the space of each month than I matured each year when I was younger.

Things will get better, but I don't think I'll ever get back to what I was. I'm not sure that I want to. I don't want to place myself in the position of taking those pills ever again. Coming off was the most horrific experience I've ever had, far worse than having my knee set after a soccer injury. The pain there was exceedingly bad, but I'd rather go through that. There's nothing I wouldn't do to get out of coming off Valium. I'd rather be hung, drawn and quartered.

DAVID AND JUDITH
One day at a time

*David, a retired minister, was left a paraplegic in
1964 after a car accident. While in hospital he was
prescribed Valium for muscle spasm and pain,
which he took continuously from 1964 until 1987.
Full recovery is a long time coming for David:
although he is no longer swamped by irrational
anger, he is still battling depression and lethargy.*

*Judith has been married to David for over thirty
years. She has supported him through all of his
trials, and speaks very honestly about the difficulties
and frustrations involved in caring for someone in
withdrawal.*

*David was put on Valium so soon after his acci-
dent that he had no time to come to terms with his
disability. Both David and Judith suspect that his
depression and anger in withdrawal have been
partly caused by the pills covering up his grief at
becoming a paraplegic.*

David

Looking back now, it seems to me I was in a fog for
years. It's hard to tell how early the tablets
started affecting me badly because I was learning to

cope with the result of the car accident – being a paraplegic – and having a small child. I had a lot of infections during that time too.

From about 1981, I felt that I was getting more and more tired. Work was hard, I didn't feel I was as alert to things. I assumed that I just wasn't working hard enough, wasn't pushing myself hard enough, wasn't concentrating enough. Quite a lot of it I blamed on myself.

I still worked, but I couldn't get over the incredible lethargy. This wasn't just mental. My body felt like it was getting heavier and heavier. I just didn't have the energy to want to do anything, even to pick up a piece of paper off the floor. I took three months' long-service leave in 1985, then six months' sick-leave in 1986, but within six months of that, I was down where I was before I'd taken either of those breaks.

I was given retirement on the basis of burn-out. I thought at the time that maybe retiring would fix me: no outside pressures, not having to work, living in a place that's nice. But it got no better, and that got me down.

I went to a specialist in allergies who put me on a particular diet, which helped but really didn't get to the heart of it. I went to a psychiatrist for quite a while.

Both the allergy doctor and the psychiatrist thought that I shouldn't be on Valium. Originally in hospital I was put on 30 mg of Valium per day, and I took the same dose daily until 1973. That year I was doing a counselling course and thought the Valium might be impairing my ability in that area, so I consulted a doctor and decided to cut the dose in half. I nearly went up the wall! That convinced me it was impossible to get off them. What I was able to do was to come down from 30 mg to 20 mg per day. I stayed on that dose until 1987.

Both doctors probably suggested I come off it, but I think due to my experience in 1973 I would have responded by telling them it just can't be done.

The psychiatrist ended by suggesting I do the Forum [a popular US 'self-actualisation' program]. Judith and I both went. I think he twigged that the drugs and the withdrawal were somehow connected with adrenalin. Something like the Forum can get your adrenalin pumping. He might have just thought that would give me a kick-start.

I didn't seek out lots of other therapies because I was just too wound down all the time. It took a lot of effort just to do the allergy doctor and psychiatrist. I think I must have been very depressed. I felt my life was winding down and I had done just about all that I was ever going to be able to.

Early in 1987 I started trying to cut down the tablets a little bit. Then in June that year I heard a woman talking on the radio about benzo dependency. I thought, this is it. So I started to come off, no second thoughts.

I just decided to cut them down by about an eighth of a tablet at a time. It took me about five or six months to come off. I got a bit impatient at the end and probably knocked off the last quarter too fast.

I made the decision to come off the tablets without consulting with my wife, so in that way it wasn't a joint project, but I think more recently in the withdrawal she has wondered if it's worth the strain. She was hoping I'd be right as soon as I came off.

Being an individual sort of a bloke and determined to come off them, I didn't need anything else really, although it was good to be able to talk to somebody if something really bizarre came up. I had contact with a support group.

How did I survive? I'd have been even more of a cot-case if I'd had to work while coming off and when pill-free. I've had to give up just about everything and concentrate totally on withdrawal.

It's hard to tell sometimes in withdrawal which of the experiences are due to the pills and which are me, particularly when I've been on them for so long. Anger has become more and more evident the further I get into withdrawal. I don't think I've ever been angry like that in the past. When I look back on it, it seems completely irrational. There's usually a trigger, but the response is quite irrational.

Just recently there was a reasonable trigger, but the anger just descended on me out of the blue. It didn't build up – I was just suddenly violently angry. I didn't know what to do with it. I went into the kitchen, put all my force behind a cabinet door, slammed it as hard as I could, and it came off its hinges. That was the minimum I could do.

I often feel angry in the night. I realise that I'm not really angry at anyone or anything. It's more like just raw anger that comes over me.

I had a dream a couple of weeks ago that I socked somebody right square in the middle of the face. The force behind my fist was absolutely monumental. I don't know who the person was. I get afraid of that in my waking life too, as though if I didn't control myself I could do something . . .

At other times I haven't done anything, but I felt that the only thing that could get rid of this anger was to break things, everything in the house. Probably what stops me is the thought of the cost and how long it would take to put things together again. So there's just a little bit of rationality somewhere.

People have been a real worry to me. Of course the most important thing in my life has been the withdrawal, and when they ask how you are, you see the curtain come down over their eyes when you start talking about it. Being in a group of people is hard, partly the noise and partly not being able to keep track of who is talking. I couldn't go to worship for about six weeks – it would have been physically and emotionally devastating to be in human company.

There are times when I feel physically beside myself, not who I am but just standing a yard to one side.

Sometimes when I'm sitting in my chair, or in bed, mostly at home, it will come over me, this awful 'Scott of the Antarctic' feeling, as though my brain is turning to water and is siphoning out of me. It's as though I've got to hold my life together; if I think another thought or feel another feeling, I'll just probably die. There's this dread that almost anything could shake my equilibrium. I've just got to hold myself in and will myself to stay alive.

A clue for coping with 'Scott of the Antarctic': place one hand across your forehead and the other hand around the back of your head. You hold your back and front brain together, as it were.

I had terrible pain in the neck and shoulders, and down my arms and back. For nearly a year, particularly getting myself out of bed and into my wheelchair, I had to be careful that I didn't fall into the gap between the bed and the chair because of the pain. But I'd say that's gone now.

The will to do things has been almost at nil at times. Fortunately, because I'm retired, I haven't had to do a great deal. Often things can be put off. Judith and I have had to come to terms with the fact that there are many things that need doing, or that we want to do, which we can't. We've missed out on quite a bit because I haven't had the will to summon up the energy to do it.

I find deadlines really awful. If there's something I have to do, it's an exertion. For example, the two services I took recently I had known about for ten weeks, and they just hung over me. I had to cancel things at times because I just couldn't put myself into thinking about anything else. In preparing for them, I knew I couldn't leave it until the last minute as I used to be able to do – I had to discipline myself.

I haven't lost the ability to care, but I've had to say, 'there are other people to take up that issue or concern'. However, the other night I had an intense sense of clarity and anticipation and really looking forward to doing something. I started to feel maybe this was what I was like as far as my thinking capacity is concerned, before I ever started on Valium. I hadn't felt like that since 1964.

It has been a help to try to remain 'even' as

much as possible and not make sudden changes in the tempo of my life. One of the big things about withdrawal for me is needing to know how others going through it are getting on. I did not find counselling particularly helpful; much better was the sharing with those whose experience is much the same as my own. My counsellor's optimism was a bit too much at times, but I did get some help from her: 'You'll get there; you'll be a better person when you get through this.'

Natural therapy practitioners helped me because they took withdrawal seriously. Orthodox medicos just disregarded withdrawal or downplayed it, saying, 'You ought to be over it by now' or 'You should exercise more.' I feel that deep controlled breathing would have been a help. Also meditation and relaxation exercises, but I seldom get around to them – the old withdrawal problem of indecision. And some meditations can be positively dangerous, especially to people as vulnerable as those in withdrawal.

I've had to accept myself, even in the times when bizarre, morbid thoughts take over or when extraordinary sexual fantasies occupy my brain. They were in the imaginative realm, not only excess of the normal, but reaching to the same gender, and bestiality. Not acted upon.

It has also been helpful to accept myself after demonstrations of anger, after outbursts of swearing, and when my self-esteem has been low. I guess that my Christian background and training have been a help here, and knowing that I am accepted as I am, not as I should be.

I'm grateful that for much of the time in withdrawal I've been able to keep hope alive – though only just at times. I think that I've been able to build up a reservoir of hope (stemming from those brief but powerful 'high' moments of withdrawal) and draw upon these. It has been important to have a hope based around what it will be like to be really and completely well.

I'm now two years and eight months off the pills. I've got the feeling now that I'm getting near the end. I felt so good and enthusiastic about doing something the other day, I could almost have gone out and told the world, It's happened – it's over. But I know you can regress. Only six weeks ago I had a fit again, but each of those seems to clear out more junk.

Someone has called withdrawal a journey out of darkness into the light, and that just about sums it up. There are still lots of bits of darkness holding on to me, but I feel that in these past two years I have seen more light than I've known for a long time. The good times are so good that I want more and more of them.

Postscript (about two years later)

Still a way to go. Just recently I had yet another bout of depression. I get tired of having a few good days only to be plunged into the black hole again. Sometimes I feel as though a cosmic travel agent is teasing me, showing me the promised land and then withholding my visa at the last moment.

But I made the decision a few weeks ago that I would now regard myself as through withdrawal, and have only a few symptoms to eliminate before ultimate health and *joie de vivre* return. The change in attitude has been a help. I'm not looking on myself as a victim any more.

At my recent sixtieth birthday party we had forty-five people. They were coming and going from five to 11 pm. How's that! I not only endured it, I positively enjoyed myself. Could you imagine me doing that three years ago?

A piece of Shakespeare has kept running through my mind as I've thought about withdrawal. I think it's this: 'As flies to wanton boys are we to the gods; they kill us for their sport.' It really does feel as though we've been tainted and played with in this time.

I want to be free of the weight that Valium has placed on me. I want to be well.

Judith

To set the scene: After twenty-two years as a paraplegic, David was forced to retire. Diagnosis, burnout. He had taken sick-leave in the hope of regaining strength but after a few months back at work he was just as bad again. The decision was made more stressful as we needed to move house as well. But the house we were moving to had to be altered first.

Finally, after six months, we were installed, and for the next six months life became steadily better for me. I'd enjoyed making some bookcases with David; I had just begun to feel I had enough energy to have friends in for the odd meal – very simple things, but life prior to retirement had become virtually work and survival, so I was relishing the decreased stress and pressure.

But not so David. He was still dogged by tiredness. I tried to assure him he'd improve in time but he wasn't convinced and was looking for an answer. It was then that he heard the program on radio about benzo withdrawal and became enthused with the idea.

I was considerably less enthused than David. While I had (in retrospect) little idea of what was ahead, I had enough sense to realise it wouldn't be easy. I was in fact quite resentful. After retirement I hadn't felt it to be as necessary to consider David's needs as carefully as when he was working. This had been a relief and gave me more freedom. Now I was having to be even more considerate of him. It felt like the last straw. I was very frustrated and disappointed.

We foolishly believed that the hardest part would be coming off the tablets. Certainly from the point of view of what I'd been hoping for from David's retirement it was bad enough, but the hope that in six months he'd be off the tablets and things would then improve sustained me.

We celebrated that event . . . felt, well, it hadn't been too bad, and looked forward to his improving. But no. Three months later he had his first fit – three in one day – and from then on for the next two years it was almost non-stop withdrawal effects.

Very few people seemed able or willing to hang in for the long haul. I learnt not to take questions about his health too seriously unless the person persisted. As I was still unravelling what it all meant myself, it wasn't surprising others didn't understand, but it was very lonely. As well as that, I felt isolated from David a lot of the time too. He was no longer able to be independent, reliable or rational in the way he'd been before. His memory was shot to pieces and it was hard not to lapse into treating him as semi-retarded or else becoming very impatient.

Because the only two tranquilliser support groups operating at that time were on the other side of Melbourne, he really wasn't well enough to travel that far, so we missed out on that support.

The fact that David actually looked better, from the point of view of people who hadn't seen him for a while, made it hard for others to appreciate how horrible he felt. He became almost totally dependent on me as his intermediary to the rest of the world (our daughters had gone overseas by this stage). One neighbour told me I must get out or I'd go under too. However, if I went out on my own, I'd come back feeling better, but David would be just as I had left him.

The pain of having to get back to where he was in order to relate to him seemed greater than staying there with him and hoping that eventually we'd come up together.

Even the pluses – improved hearing, sight, etcetera – were often a source of strain as he tended to go right over the top. I felt left behind in a somewhat less exciting world, but I knew I needed to stay there to support him when he inevitably came back with a thud.

I finally realised that I had to make decisions based on whether I felt I could manage what was involved. But only after some disastrous experiences resulting from acceding to his persistent requests to do things he just couldn't see through, and which left us both in tatters. I found myself assuming the role of being in charge – something I didn't enjoy at all.

Thanks to Valium, much of David's grief over the losses from the accident had been glossed over. Now they came out with a vengeance. This naturally rekindled my own grief at having my husband become a paraplegic. Even the skills he'd acquired to compensate for his disability – getting in and out of his chair, bed, the car with relative ease – now became burdensome, chores that seemed to take all his will. He began complaining endlessly about these daily tasks and this was very wearing.

We've had some absolutely humdinger arguments. I felt a pig to be arguing with someone so unwell and so stretched to his limit, but I'd become so desperate I wouldn't know what to do. A few times we felt we would not be able to stick together – indeed we wondered if we were actually making each other worse. But somehow we'd recover and begin again.

One of the greatest lessons Valium has taught me is that elimination of pain is not helpful unless at the same time the cause of the pain is being addressed. This applies whether the pain is physical or emotional. It has also taught me to be sceptical about drugs in general and the extravagant claims that are often made. When I hear of a new drug with all sorts of wonderful properties I immediately think, but what are the side-effects? The belief in, and gratitude for, natural therapies has only increased.

What kept me going? David's belief that he

would eventually come through was almost constantly present and while I had little real hope, his
hope did help me hang on. The natural therapists we
consulted were a great support. The feeling that,
horrible and all as it was, I was painfully learning difficult but important lessons about life. The fact
that we could devote much of our attention and
energy to what we needed. It has taken all we had,
but we could never have managed it if either of us
had to hold down a job. My Christian faith which
was often barely enough to save me from desperation. The community of the Church and a few
friends who, while not knowing what to do, com-
municated they really cared. The garden. Our
family – although long distance parted us, we
know they cared.

Has it been worth it? I hope one day I may be
able to say, yes, but certainly not yet. I don't feel I'm
yet back to where I was seven years ago, and that
wasn't great. In some ways David is better, in
others not as well. He still feels tired much of the
time with many symptoms persisting, albeit much
less acutely. We press on as best we can. We talk
and reflect a lot. We're still learning to listen more
closely to our whole body needs and be considerate
of ourselves and each other.

JACKIE
Prisoner in her own house

Jackie is a cheerful, outgoing woman in her mid-forties. As well as caring for her husband and two children she works full-time as a secretary. Her story illustrates how benzodiazepines can induce anxiety symptoms even when prescribed for physical ailments. Jackie was first put on benzos for irritable bowel syndrome in the early 1980s. Within a short time she became so agoraphobic that she could hardly leave her house. She has been off benzos for nearly six years and considers herself to be completely recovered.

I tried to analyse the reasons I first started taking benzos, thinking, how did I get started on all this? My health was fine – in fact I was rather a well person. I certainly never thought of myself as nervous. I always played a lot of sport, and very rarely visited the doctor except for the yearly check-up.

My mother-in-law died of cancer a couple of years before my second daughter was born, about 1979. It was rather traumatic for us all, but we coped, and life went on normally, as before.

After I had Kelly in 1981 I started having trouble with my bowels – a mixture of diarrhoea and constipation. I was a bit worried about this because my mother-in-law had died of bowel cancer, and I started to think, oh gosh, I wonder if I've really got something wrong with me? I went to the doctor who said he didn't think it was anything too serious – if I ate more fibre it would be fine. I did that but it didn't go away, and I had a niggling suspicion in my head – if everything was all right why didn't it go away? The doctor sent me for various tests and then to a specialist to reassure me. I had a sigmoidoscopy, which was fine, but he said I had an irritable bowel syndrome. He gave me some Librax tablets [benzos] to take. I took three courses and they were really good; they cleared up my problem.

I'd returned to work part-time when all of a sudden I started to get these really strange panic feelings at the office, for no reason. I was frightened – I didn't know why. Of course that worried me. I rang my husband and said, 'I feel really sick' – I explained it as being sick but in fact I just wanted to get home. He came and drove me home from work. I had a chance of a full-time job; I accepted it and then knocked it back because that first panic attack made me afraid to get out. I was nervous about going out on my own. That just developed – it became horrendous.

I worried about why I had those funny feelings, so I went to a doctor who was close by and he said, 'You've got a toddler and you're a bit run down – you're probably just a little bit stressed, but don't worry about it – take these.' I then got my first prescription for Serepax.

I finished the course and then I stopped. I thought I'd be fine. Next morning I decided to take myself to the local shopping mall – and there I had a worse panic attack than I'd ever had before. I went straight back to the doctor and said, 'I hate feeling the way I do, I don't like being out on my own.' He gave me another prescription and said I just needed to take them a bit longer. So I took them a bit longer, and a bit longer, and a bit longer – and three years down the track I was still taking Serepax.

I hardly ever saw my doctor – he would write the prescription for me or even put it in to the chemist. I took them just like you take antibiotics. I have never finished a full course of antibiotics in my whole life, but I was never without those tablets. I was panic-stricken if I didn't have them in my bag.

Something must have said, 'God, Jackie, there is something wrong here', so I tried to cut down a few times – but of course it's useless. I used to feel so ashamed of taking the pills when my husband or the kids were around. I'd sneak them – I don't know why. I'd take them very surreptitiously.

Soon after I started on Serepax I developed real agoraphobia. I would sit on this couch all day – I wouldn't move out of it. It got to the stage where I wouldn't go and get the mail or peg washing on the line. I'd go out with my husband, but under real duress – I'd have to take a Serepax and keep it in the bag – I never felt comfortable. I didn't see the pills as my problem at that stage; I saw the agoraphobia as the problem.

I was up to seven tablets a day and I was still sitting on the couch. I wasn't taking any interest in the kids. One day I was crying, so Mum rang my husband at work and said he'd have to come home. I didn't know what to do – I thought I was going to end up in a psychiatric ward. I had lost the plot of it all, I couldn't work out how to get my life back in control. My husband told me, 'It must be the tablets, it's got to be the tablets! You're not like this normally – I knew you before these drugs and nothing's happened that would make you like this.'

During the time I was on benzos I also got very headachey and had menstrual problems. My bowels were still playing up but I didn't worry about that any more. I took a lot of tests – I had brain scans, CAT scans, thyroid tests – you name it, I had every test. I thought I had multiple sclerosis. I said to my husband one day, 'How much money do you think we spent on doctors when I was on tranquillisers?' He said, 'Well, since you've been off our bank balance is a lot healthier.' I was at the doctors at least once a week.

I took tranquillisers for five years, starting with the Librax, the bulk of the time on Serepax and finishing with Xanax. I came off the pills in hospital, as an in-patient. It took me five weeks. One of the nurses in the hospital told me that my problems started with that first prescription of Librax. It was prescribed as a relaxant for the bowel, and it obviously helped that – I didn't have the muscle spasm or the pain. I'd taken those tablets, and he'd given me two repeats to make sure that I was okay. But Librax is another benzodiazepine, and because I hadn't taken many drugs at all in my life, a little amount would probably have affected me quite a lot. That's what the panic attack was at work.

During the early months of withdrawal I classified a day as a great day when I got up, had a shower and got dressed. I lost about a stone and a half. I've got a picture of myself and my shoulder blades are sticking out. My face was really drawn – but I think that's normal for the first three months. There were so many symptoms, but my biggest problem apart from the agoraphobia was the terrible free-floating anxiety that would come and go for no reason. I'd be sitting perfectly happy watching TV, and then all of a sudden I'd be fearful. It wasn't caused by anything.

I can feel anxious now but I know that anxiety is a quite okay thing to feel. There are things I have been through in the last two years that if I was a 'neurotic' woman I'd have been back on those pills without a shadow of a doubt. Last year my daughter was attacked by two bulldogs and she needed eighty stitches in her leg. She was a real mess. I was with her – she was rollerskating when these dogs went for her legs and I couldn't get them off. I was screaming. I was very anxious then, and very frightened, and very stressed out – but it was okay to be exactly like that.

The free-floating anxiety lasted about two years and then just gradually went away. Now when I feel anxious there's some reason for it.

Most of the time I was on the pills I stayed home. I couldn't leave, I couldn't drive anywhere. I tried to do a part-time job working for a vet not far away, and for a while it was all right. Something inside me kept wanting to get back to my normal life, and because I kept failing all the time, I then stopped trying to go for jobs and to carry on. I thought I was having a nervous breakdown – some psychiatric problem, and that I would never be a normal person again.

I started a new job a month before I came off the pills. It was a secretarial job just across the road – I only had to walk to the corner. I was getting to the stage where I really couldn't manage it – I couldn't think straight. The typing was very difficult because I was slow, and I wasn't used to that. I've done a lot of secretarial work before, in very high-powered jobs. I was secretary to a general manager, and so I had to deal with people at the higher management level, and also the reps under them.

But while I was doing that job my self-esteem was growing as well. It had been at rock-bottom, but I figured that as long as I could keep in the job I would become Jackie again, because Jackie was capable of holding down a secretarial job. I wasn't Ian's wife and I wasn't the girls' mother – I was Jackie, and that was what I wanted.

The first morning I went back to work I had the shakes so badly that I couldn't hold the tooth-brush properly – my husband had to clean my teeth for me. Mum watched me walk out the door. She said, 'You stood at the side gate for ages and ages. I was going to go out, and I thought, no, I won't. I was sure you were going to walk back in that gate and say you weren't going to work – but you walked. It took you at least ten minutes and you finally decided you'd walk across.' And I did. Once I got to work I was fine. In a way it was a lifesaver. I knew I had to work because I had made a commitment. There were times when I felt a bit lousy but it kept me occupied; it filled my day.

The anxiety and agoraphobia improved slowly and gradually. The headaches, muscle spasm and shakes were erratic. Those symptoms came and went till all of a sudden they didn't come any more. I had some very good days when I felt really great. On those days I'd try to do as much as I could. I remember once we'd been out on a Sunday and it was absolutely brilliant, and I thought, this is normal. Then later on during that week I was so far back into withdrawal it was unbelievable. I was sitting on the couch thinking that I really hadn't progressed very far. Then my daughter came in with my diary, and said, 'Mum, you're worried because you've got your headaches and aches and pains back. Why don't you just read back about what we did on Sunday?'

I took that withdrawal diary with me every-where – just a little exercise book. I took it with me to the cricket about six months after I came off the pills. Just the thought of going to the MCG when I was on pills would have freaked me right out – all those people and nowhere to go. My husband went off to the loo and to get a hotdog. I was sitting alone in this huge space surrounded by 80,000 people, and I felt so frightened. So I got my diary out and started writing! I wrote things like, 'The man in front of me looks really nice, I could start a conversation with him', and 'My husband will be back soon.' I looked at it the other day and I laughed and thought what a nutcase I was, writing in a diary in the middle of the MCG. It was part of a conscious effort all the time to tell myself not to be frightened and to relax.

For the first four years I think every symptom I had was as a result of withdrawal. You go through too much hard work to get your life back under control and to start doing the things you want to do to have them tell me, okay, maybe these things are caused by problems before you went on the pills. No way am I going to accept that. I remember the person I was then, and I'm more like that person now. I know I'm back to the old Jackie. We're going through a really stressful time at the moment with my mum – she's really ill. If I was that neurotic person I would be a wreck at the moment – and I'm not. I feel miserable, and I could cry sometimes when I look at her – but it's not going to set me back. It's not withdrawal – it's a healthy feeling of sadness.

There are too many labels around, and that's where the problem comes from – people are told they are 'a neurotic' or they're anxious. If I am labelled I will end up turning into my label and I'm not going to do that. I'm going to feel happy, I'm going to feel depressed, I'm going to feel deliriously excited, but it will all be a purely natural thing that's coming from me the person, not a drug that I've put in my body. I think I should be able to own the feelings I have, and they are totally different to the ones I had when I was on the pills.

I believe you should be totally honest about withdrawal. To me the horror story is being on the pills – withdrawal is tough, but not the horror story my life was on those pills. Someone coming off pills and going through withdrawal isn't a horror story – it's a success story. Someone is taking back control over their lives and managing without something to help them along. You may not be symptom-free, but you're getting better. If you continue to take the pills you are not getting better, you are stagnating or getting worse, because soon that level will not be enough, and you will have to increase your dosage to cope.

These days I don't take anything without asking about the side-effects. If the doctors aren't prepared to answer me then I don't take anything. I go somewhere else. I guess I've learnt a lesson, but it was a hard way to learn it. I never thought a doctor would do anything to harm me, and I'm not saying they did willingly, but there's got to be alternatives. About four months into withdrawal I went back to my GP and told him I wasn't taking the things any more. I didn't need them, I was driving around – it wasn't easy, but each day I'd got a little bit better. He said, 'I think mentally you're healthier now.' I said, 'No – I came hoping that you won't put another woman on these pills.' He said they were a very good drug and have a very good use. I said, 'Yes, but not for five years! Maybe for a week or two, but not for that long.'

He really couldn't see what I was trying to get at.

SEAN
Teaching career in ruins

Sean, now in his early fifties, was put on Valium in 1970 following a life crisis. He loved his work as a country primary school teacher, but a troubled relationship and overcrowding in his classroom led to a stress-related breakdown – and his first prescription for Valium. Trying to deal with the benzo symptoms led to too much alcohol.

Sean had an unusually long withdrawal. Even after eleven years off pills he still has some symptoms left, what he calls 'a legacy of bits and pieces'.

I lost my mother when I was two years old and my father when I was five. I was brought up by a maiden aunt and she was very good, but you never replace your parents. When I look back, I realise that I was depressed for all my childhood. There was just something there – a deep loneliness – you didn't know what it was.

I think it was a fear of loss that caused my breakdown. My wife-to-be had been having an affair just before we were married. I found this out when I was under a lot of pressure at school – I was a teacher. I had a rural school with only sixteen children, and the numbers were increased to forty in six months. There was only one room and I was trying to teach – I had to climb over desks to get to the kids. It was criminal really. They gave me another teacher in the end, but we still only had one classroom – a tiddly little country classroom. I was under a lot of pressure and I snapped a bit, I suppose, and became agitated and very confused, and that was the start of the Valium.

The local doctor prescribed the pills. They calmed me down for a while, but I was so confused at that stage I didn't know what was going on. It didn't improve but I think I was over-treated. I was eventually sent to a state psychiatrist and he put me in hospital for about ten days.

They gave me brain scans and put me on Lithium and that really knocked me around. They also put me on anti-depressants in that period. I stayed on those drugs for a year, trying each one out, but they were poisonous to me. I felt so crook and out of myself that I decided to give them up. I had been told that I would have to stay on some of these medications for the rest of my life.

I was still going downhill. Apart from the stay in hospital, I was working all the time, which was difficult. I had two weeks off – I should have taken more. They couldn't work out what was wrong with me. I took the Valium for six years. Then a 'magic' new thing called Serepax was offered to me. I was told that it was non-addictive and had no side-effects, a perfectly safe tablet. That was in 1976. I took it for several years.

The Valium was helpful for a while, as was the Serepax. I took the pills according to how I felt. If I didn't have one in the morning I was a dithering mess – I would have to have it. Then I would settle down and feel all right. At lunchtime I'd start to tense up and start fidgeting again. I'd need another one, then I would settle down. I thought that was what I was like – my nerves had broken down to that extent and these tablets were doing me good. I couldn't survive without the damn things. I was taking four a day regularly but it edged up to eight depending on how I felt. The prescribed dose was up to three a day, I think. I had no problem getting tablets.

After about six months on Serepax I started to get panic attacks. I'd be standing in front of a class and I'd suddenly freeze, my heart would race. I thought I was dying – having a heart attack. I'd never been nervous in front of a class before.

I also noticed that just as I was going off to sleep, I'd come fully awake with a start, with palpitations and a racing heart. I'd have to talk to myself, tell myself that I was in my own bed – I know where I am. It was a terrifying sensation – it made me afraid to go to sleep. The room used to spin or rock. I'd have to get up and do something to calm myself – I thought I was going to die. That still happens sometimes. The sensation is that I don't know where I am, but I do.

I became very agoraphobic, very, very much so – scared that I'd fall flat on my face or do something silly. I always walked on the inside of the footpath so that if one of these attacks came I could grab something to save myself from falling and making a real goat of myself.

I started to lose all my confidence and became a

virtual hermit. I lost my impetus, my drive. I couldn't be bothered, I didn't want to do things. I wanted to curl up in a corner and stay out of things. I really had to push myself just to get out of the house. If I wasn't stubborn I'd really have gone downhill but I fought myself all the time – I wasn't going to let the damn thing beat me. I forced myself to go into situations even where I knew I'd have a panic attack to see if I could overcome it.

I thought these symptoms must have been caused by some major illness – I didn't know what. I saw a number of doctors but they wouldn't listen; they just wanted to put me on more drugs. I told them I wouldn't take any other drugs. I thought I was happy on Serepax.

I was put on sick-leave after the first few panic attacks. I still didn't know what was wrong with me. I started using alcohol to calm me and help me sleep. One night I took four or five extra Serepax to help me sleep – but it didn't. I must have got up and gone down the street to the pub and had a few beers and then driven home again. I had no intention whatsoever of driving. As a result, I cleaned up a shop-front and lost my licence for about two years. I don't remember a thing about it – frightening. Thank Christ no one was hurt.

I was superannuated in 1979. Those pills really stuffed my life up – they really did. It was a dark time.

Then one day I was listening to a program on the radio which said that they were starting to get information that Serepax can be as addictive as heroin. I was shocked. I'm dead against drugs; I only take them because I have to. I thought to myself, if that bloody stuff is like heroin I'm not going to take it. If they reckon I'm addicted – well, I'm not going to be. I just stopped dead cold. The main thing that stands out, looking back, is that I wanted to get off the things and I was going to do it – that was paramount. I did. And did I suffer for it.

My life was totally disrupted. My wife left at one stage, and I lost most of my friends. I could talk to my brother about the physical aspects of with-drawal, as he is a doctor and ten years older than me, but I had no one I could discuss the emotional side with, and God knows I needed someone.

I was anxious all the time for years after coming off the pills. It was an all-encompassing worry, a tightness – an overwhelming fear. It is only in the last few years that I have felt better. I am not scared of anyone or anything much, so this was awful for me. I've had pet snakes and climbed mountains – it never worried me. But the fear within myself was the thing I couldn't cope with. It was irrational. I would say to myself, I'm not scared of anything and yet I'm suffering from this terrible fear.

I used to get bloody awful panic attacks. They'd come on at any time. You might be watching TV, and you suddenly feel a tenseness. You think, watch out, here we go again. You twig straight away and try to focus on something else. It starts to build up in intensity, you start to hyperventilate, your heart starts racing. You feel immense and overwhelming fear, like the fear of death. You have to get up and do something else, just move yourself, like go outside and sit on the porch, to take your mind off it – to divert yourself from what you are experiencing. If you can do that, quite often after two or three minutes the thing will go. Then I might light a pipe to bring myself back down to get over it.

I had rotten depression too while I was on the pills and for a long time after I came off – for about six years. You feel yourself going – you know you are going to get in a depressive state and you just can't do anything about it. I was quite suicidal a few times. I couldn't see the point of living – it was a dead-end at that time. I had a full bottle of pills and I thought that would do it. I quaffed the whole lot with a bottle of beer and then I staggered into bed. I thought, ah, that's it, finished, the end. You have no idea the peace I felt. And then I woke up the next bloody morning and I still went to teach! I wasn't crook enough to stay home.

I didn't take anything for the depression. I fought it myself. It was a matter of kicking yourself in the pants and getting going again.

My sex life was buggered up as well. Physically it was often an impossibility. I'd be stimulated mentally but nothing would happen, which was very frustrating. When I did have sex I'd feel sick afterwards. Even now if the sex is very emotionally charged I feel sick afterwards. It is not very pleasant for anyone if you have jumped around and had a hell of a good time and then have to race for the bathroom. It is not good for the relationship.

I eventually got back together with my wife and kid, but my wife still doesn't understand. The greatest battle was for her to understand what I was feeling. I got her several books to read and she wouldn't even read the bloody things. In the end I accepted the fact that she wasn't going to understand. I just did things myself because I wasn't going to lose my kid – I worked my way around that one and she still doesn't know a hell of a lot about it but we are living together fairly well now. I think that is due mainly to me getting off the Serepax and more or less coming to grips with myself again.

Gardening helped me – that was the best thing I had. I sat outside with my tomatoes – I found it calming. I couldn't read, as I had lost my concentration. There wasn't much I could do, because I couldn't concentrate even to go fishing. I don't think I'm fully recovered; I don't think I'll ever be fully recovered.

I'm still left with these little bits and pieces – the legacy of it. I'm still a bit agoraphobic, I don't like crowded places. I can go shopping more easily now at times which are less crowded. I couldn't go to a cricket match or a concert. I was not like this before I started taking the pills. I didn't particularly like crowds, but this really worries me. It's certainly got better – for example I can drive into the city, which I could never do.

I don't know how much better I'm going to get though. I feel as though I'm on a plateau. It's basically a lack of confidence, a need to be alone in a noiseless cocoon. I now enjoy life much more, not completely, but not like it was before, when I was on the pills. Life was an effort then.

MARIA
Young woman on the go

Maria was a lively, healthy young woman in her mid-twenties when she was first prescribed Serepax for minor stress symptoms. This led to six years of addiction, and a merry-go-round of psychiatrists and psychologists. Looking back she is sure that benzos affected her chances of forming relationships and prevented her from leading a normal life. Now in her mid-thirties, and five years off benzos, she is completely recovered and looks forward with optimism to making up for the years she lost.

I had been working very hard and I had some heart palpitations, so I went to the doctor. She asked me if I was stressed out. I thought I was no more stressed than the next person. I said I had a few problems at home and I worked hard, but I really thought the problem was something physical.

She gave me 7 mg of Serepax to take twice a day. I didn't really notice any difference for the first couple of days that I took it, so I went back and said I was just the same – no energy and I was still having heart palpitations. I would get on the tram and my heart would be really beating wildly. I was scared I was having a heart attack. I was twenty-seven then.

The doctor referred me to a psychiatrist but she didn't tell me what she thought was wrong with me. She had written a letter to him. I thought, I'm not going to pass this over without reading it. So I did and I was really cross when I read it. She had written 'acute anxiety'. I thought that I had something physical – I didn't think I was anxious!

So I go to the psychiatrist. He starts taking a history – family and all that. He decides to increase my dose of Serepax to 30 mg twice a day. So I thought, he knows what he is doing.

I took it and I started to feel weird – crying for no reason – really angry for no reason. I'd be at work and it would really get to me. I started to feel dizzy all the time and I had other strange symptoms.

The smaller dose didn't affect me at all but I got sick very quickly after being prescribed the 30 mg twice a day.

I kept going back to him thinking that there must definitely be something wrong with me now. After what the doctor had written and getting all the odd symptoms I started to believe I had become an 'acutely anxious' person. The symptoms became magnified and that made me think I was falling apart.

It wasn't as if I'd not been trying to help myself. I really wanted to relax more so when one of the girls at work said, 'Let's go and do some yoga', I went along. But because I was taking the tablets it didn't do anything, so after a while I gave it up. I had been going to the psychiatrist for about two and a half months at that time. He thought that there was some underlying reason for my anxiety, such as problems at home. I couldn't understand what he meant because it wasn't that bad at home – maybe if I stayed out too late Dad would pick on me, but I didn't feel there was anything in particular that was really worrying me at the time. I kept putting the symptoms down to too much stress at work because I was young and I had to manage a staff of three.

I didn't like the psychiatrist so I went back to my GP. She kept writing scripts for Serepax for about two years, without me ever going to the surgery. I would ring her, say I needed another prescription for Serepax and she would say, just pick it up in an hour.

I took the pills for about two years not knowing why, but I felt yucky if I didn't. I never once increased the dose during this period. I used to feel guilty about taking them, so I went to different chemists. I worried they would think I was a 'druggy'. I remember that I got really angry at one chemist because he gave me a bigger dosage. I went back and said, in a really cross voice, 'I don't need a bigger dosage, thanks.'

I kept trying to find someone to help me relax. Eventually I found a psychologist who practised hypnotherapy. He kept telling me that the tablets that I was on were not good for me and that I should stop taking them. The hypnotherapy did help a bit, it calmed me down and I then took less Serepax. I was able to cut the dose in half, so for another year and a half it was 30 mg a day. Then for a short time – about a week – I tried to cut the dose down even further to 7 mg per day but I went all crazy and weird, so I went back to 30 mg per day.

I still wasn't okay. I was referred to another psychiatrist and she told me that the tablets were not good for me – she made me feel guilty for taking them. She said that she could put me in hospital to come off them. I was starting to panic: I didn't want to go into hospital. I didn't think I was sick enough to go into a psychiatric ward. I was very confused about what I should be doing by then. I had lost my ability to follow through and make decisions.

That psychiatrist sent me to a psychologist as well – I was having group therapy – it cost me a fortune. I didn't like the therapy at all, as it was all about touching and being close. These people were on anti-depressants and all sorts of mind-altering drugs. I was only on tranquillisers, I didn't feel I should be there – I didn't want to be part of that group. I said that to her.

About that time I saw a program about tranquillisers on TV. As I watched it all the hairs on the back of my neck stood on end, and I realised, that is me! Everything dropped into place and I knew that I had to do something about it, so I wrote down the telephone number of the agency mentioned in the program. I didn't do anything about it for a while because I was so embarrassed that – there was my life on TV. You know that this is you – you are taking these pills and you are addicted. I kept saying the word, 'addicted'.

I rang up and cancelled my next appointment with the psychiatrist. I said, 'Look, this will be the last time I will be seeing you, because, frankly, I don't think you're helping me. And this group therapy is not helping me. I think it is the drugs that are making me feel like this.'

I had decided to see a counsellor at the agency which helps people come off benzos. I had rung them and been told that my symptoms were being caused by the pills. I knew then that I could be like I used to be – when you know what the enemy is you can take some action. I had been doing everything I could think of to get better but I was getting worse; I really thought I was becoming a very anxious person. My parents didn't know anything – I was embarrassed about taking the pills, so I never told them until I was coming off them because I had to take time off work. I never went to the GP after that time. I had been on the pills for six years.

It took me a while to cut down to the last scrap of pill. I was frightened to come off because the pills had become such a crutch. But in the end, all the symptoms I had coming off the pills I had been having anyway, so it made no difference, on or off!

I decided to take my long-service leave. I'm a office manager in public relations – I do everything – I have been there such a long time, for sixteen years. I completely withdrew, even at work. I delegated a lot of my work out – I just said, you do that. My boss was really understanding and took a lot of the work off me. He said that he knew what I was going through because his wife had been through it. She had been in hospital and they put her on benzos for a short time, but even so she developed a lot of the symptoms.

I worked part-time for six months – but I couldn't

do anything else. During the weekends I really withdrew. I didn't do any driving. My sister, who is on part-time work at the same place, drove me to and from work. I couldn't drive, in fact I still have trouble driving. Some mornings I can do it and others I can't – it's crazy! I'm not too bad as long as it's not peak-hour traffic.

For ages my head was not clear – I couldn't think – it was woolly, encased. I also got this terrible feeling as though someone had put my head in a paper bag and they were rattling it. I am still having head symptoms. Some mornings I feel fantastic – I wash my hair, put on a good dress and I'm fine. I get to work but by the afternoon I have this terrible headache.

I had ringing in my ears – I still have that. I had this awful metallic taste – it was like chewing the silver paper on the chewing gum. I was really yellow but I didn't know I was until I saw some photos.

I rarely have a normal bowel motion, and had an awful bladder problem. I used to go all the time – it was terrible. I had no control over it. Everywhere I went I would check out the toilets because I couldn't hold onto the water. I used to panic. I have more control over it now.

I lost weight on the tablets and then I gained two stone which I have lost recently by dieting. I used to eat to make myself feel better. Mum used to cook and I would eat – there was no stopping me. This 'machine' was eating all the time. I didn't seem to care that I was gaining weight. I let myself go – I dressed in black, and I usually care about the way I look.

I felt dead sexually – I couldn't have got it together even if I had wanted to for the first few years. Then I became really sexually turned-on. It just comes really suddenly – you just want to – 'whoo'. I think, wouldn't I like to . . . It's embarrassing. I think that I shouldn't be having these thoughts. One day at work I said, 'You know what I could use right now?' They were all laughing at me thinking I was going to say something to eat, and I said, 'A good fuck.' And they go, 'Maria!' I was really embarrassed when I realised what I had said, but sometimes I get really randy and I think, control yourself!

I haven't had a man in my life for a long time and that depresses me. I start feeling that I've missed out because of these pills. You don't allow anyone to get close in withdrawal – you build this little barrier around you. Someone might say you are really attractive and you say to yourself, no way, I'm not really attractive. You won't accept it. Like guys at work tell me I'm looking really good and I just pass it off.

I still have a lot of tiredness – it's an unnatural tiredness. I walk to my car for ten minutes and it always brings on symptoms. And within the first couple of weeks of taking pills I became agoraphobic and claustrophobic. I didn't know what was happening to me.

Even now, there are days when it is really freaky – when I have to walk against the wall. Walk where there are a lot of buildings – where there is not a lot of open space.

I often feel that the ground is moving. I still wear shoes with a rubber sole – it's like, if I have a better grip on the ground I won't fall over – it is really weird. I am a long way from recovered in this area. Some mornings I feel like wearing runners and other mornings I can wear high-heeled shoes because I'm okay. But I don't seem to have so much of a problem if I am in an area which I know – say home or work. It is when I go to somewhere where I have no control over the environment – like shopping centres.

I get bruises all the time. I have them all over. I found a lot on my legs and on my backside and I never remembered hitting myself. Anxiety is with me all the time too – some days good, some days bad. Some days I can talk to the managing director with no problems and other days, even to say a word to him, I will shy away – I won't speak to him in case he asks me a question and I get anxious about it. It is worse than it was before I was on tablets but not as bad as when I was first coming off. But I don't have panic attacks now.

The symptoms have been going away very gradually but they're erratic. One day I'm sick and then the next I can be feeling a little better. Then you can slip right back. For instance, I felt much better a few months ago than I do now. However, I had a really good day yesterday. You get discouraged and you think, I'm back here again. It is like you have failed in some way. You need someone to tell you that it is withdrawal so you don't blame yourself for something you have no control over. It's crazy. Overall though, I'm very much better now than when I was on the pills.

If I get up in the morning and I have symptoms, there is nothing I can do about it – it just has to run its course. I make sure I don't have to rush – that brings on symptoms. I didn't tell many people what was wrong with me – I just dropped out of sight. I don't tell people now, at this stage. You have to pretend you are all right.

Getting the information about what the benzos do to you is what helped me to come off my pills. TV and videos helped me to get through the worst of the withdrawal. I couldn't read because I couldn't concentrate, and the radio used to drive me bananas. At first I used to watch everything on TV – everything was okay. It helped me to keep my mind off my symptoms. I used to watch all the soaps but I would be a million miles away – I wouldn't really be watching them. I became a couch potato – that was where the weight gain came on.

I feel that I have had six years taken out of my life. I had a lot of trouble feeling anything very much. There was no excitement – I felt flat all the time. I did things mechanically. I went on two holidays and they were terrible because I was sick, anxious and unhappy. You're supposed to feel better when you go on a holiday, but I felt worse. I'm now thinking about going away again because I feel I am getting well enough to enjoy a holiday. I'm really excited about the thought of it.

Coming off the pills was the hardest thing I have ever done. You lose your friends because you cannot go out with them. One good thing is that I did save money in the first two years coming off the pills because I didn't shop. I am going to spend it now. I know I'm a long way from being well and I still have to fight with all my emotions and all that, but it is worth it to know that you are getting better and you are feeling real feelings.

I have now been off pills for two and a half years and I would say I am about three-quarters recovered. I hope I will recover completely but there is a little twinge of fear that some symptoms may stay with me. I am still a little agoraphobic and I am frightened that it might stay. It was really worth coming off the pills. It was the best thing that happened to me – it was a turning point.

OLIVER
Benzos helped the show go on

Oliver is a professional entertainer. He is seventy-two, very fit, and still performing regularly. He took benzodiazepines for two short periods, many years apart, because of nervous exhaustion. The Valium was very helpful – it got him through the bad patches. Oliver is an example of someone who took benzos for a few months and was able to come off without a problem.

I took Valium for a short time during the 1970s. At that time I was suffering from severe nervous exhaustion. I was working very hard, very long hours, and travelling a lot. I got to the stage in my act where I couldn't think what I was going to say, couldn't think what I was going to come up with next. It affected my speech while I was performing. I used to only last about half an hour in a conversation and then I'd get all itchy and nervy and my voice would go funny. I think that it was nervous exhaustion. As well as that I had a hyperactive son and I wasn't getting much sleep. I felt as though a hand had pulled all my insides out and I had nothing to go on with.

I went to the doctor who prescribed a tonic and 2 mg of Valium after every meal. The Valium worked well – calmed me down but didn't make me feel drowsy. I took it for maybe a couple of months. It helped me a lot, particularly with my nervous speech difficulties. It wasn't hard to take – not a nasty medicine but just a little tablet which was easy to swallow. I took it intermittently – if I felt I was going to have one of the attacks, I'd just take one and within half an hour I'd be feeling fine, like I'm feeling now. I could drive my car, carry on a normal conversation without thinking about what I was going to say. Then I decided I didn't need them any more. So I gave them away without a problem.

Some years later I was working in a kids' show for Honey Week, performing with all the bees. In the middle of the show I felt dreadful and thought I was going to have another one of those attacks. In fact I was afraid I was going to have a heart attack. I hurried the show up and went to a hospital. They gave me a full medical on the spot but found nothing wrong with me and could only put it down to nervous exhaustion.

Once again they recommended Valium, but put me on a much higher dose than the local doctor had. I was told to take two after every meal. I didn't think I needed that many, so I didn't do what the doctor said – I just took one when I needed it.

Then one night, a few months later, I was out at a church dinner and I thought to myself, I don't need these any more, and I stopped taking them. I haven't taken them since. I don't think I could have been addicted to them. I used to keep two or three with me as a back-up when I was doing shows, just in case.

I must say in all fairness to the drug that I don't think I'd have got by without it. What it did was calm me down and make me feel normal. I don't so much thank Valium, but it did get me through.

JULIA
Family's life put on hold

Julia is in her mid-sixties – an intelligent, energetic woman. She took heart surgery in her stride, but the sleeping pills she was given in hospital led to her first panic attack. Later she was put on Ativan and Normison. Although she took them for less than a year, it was enough to induce alarming symptoms. Julia's main problems were her severe and bizarre head symptoms and her crippling depression. Her main regret is how badly the pills affected her family life. She found it hard to communicate with her children and grandchildren, and eventually her marriage broke up.

Some days I feel so isolated; my pain isolates me. When I'm like that I can't go to bowls, I can't visit my grandchildren, I can't walk up the street and talk to people. I've got to crawl inside myself. In the film *Being There* with Peter Sellers, they all thought he was wise and he wasn't; he was just sitting watching – and that's what I'm like. The Julia that I used to know, she's treading water, waiting for all this to go so that she can then resume her life.

Four years ago I felt very well. I had a full-time job

as well as looking after my husband and children. My daughter was having her first baby and I went down every week to do the washing and cleaning because she had high blood-pressure. I took over her household and I was running my own.

Then suddenly I needed heart surgery – for my arteries actually, my heart is fine. I was given sleeping pills in hospital and took the bottle home with me. I took them until they ran out. At first in recuperation I was fine, but as the months went on I got increasingly nervous. I couldn't understand it. I began having what I now know were slight panic attacks, and my husband got me into the cardiac rehabilitation hospital. The director took my blood pressure and did all the physical things, then sent a young doctor with some pills. She said, 'This is the only medication he will prescribe.' It was Ativan. I didn't know what it was at the time. But of course it was a tranquilliser.

At night the hospital staff gave me two Normison to help me sleep. They made me dead groggy every morning. I often used to sleep in the day – no one questioned it. This was an immediate effect of the pills.

I was in that hospital for six weeks. The day before I went home I asked the nurse whether I could possibly be addicted to these tablets. 'Oh no, dear, no,' she said. I swallowed them, and within twenty minutes I could have backed a truck down that ward and not touched a bed, I was so calm. Next morning the cardiac specialist was by my bed at 6 am. He took a foolscap sheet of notes. I asked him about the Normison and he said, 'I don't know, my dear; refer it to your local doctor.'

When I left, the pharmacist gave me a bottle of Ativan and a bottle of Normison with no warning whatsoever. I never had a prescription for a benzo. I became addicted without having a prescription. I took them continuously for a further six weeks and after that spasmodically for five months.

At that time my general health seemed to be all right. My recovery from heart surgery was proceeding well. Physically I was fine but psychologically I was down the drain. I began to feel quite nervous, and I thought, this is extraordinary, I'm becoming more nervous than I was before. I noticed that I wasn't handling things; I would yell at my husband and I would break down and cry.

In my ignorance, one day I tossed aside the Ativan and the Normison. Two days later when I woke up I had this incredible feeling in my head. My brain was split – one side of it was jumping up and down and the other side was going to sleep, as if it was dying. I wasn't worried about the side that was jumping, I was worried about the side that was dying. I thought I'd had a stroke. I called my husband to get me to the hospital. They rang a cardiac man, put me on an ECG machine, did blood tests straight away. Two hours later they said I wasn't having a stroke or a heart attack and put me in intensive care. It cost me seven hundred dollars for one night plus all the doctors' fees.

I was certain that I was addicted to the pills and that they were causing all my problems. I went back to see the director of the cardiac hospital who first gave me the drugs. He just ridiculed me. He said, 'How did we arrive at that diagnosis, my dear?' But I was sure I was right. I decided to come off them.

I found two doctors who understood about tranquilliser withdrawal. They changed me over to Valium and reduced my dose very, very slowly. It took about four months to come right off. I have been off the pills now for two years and five months.

By far my worst withdrawal symptom was headaches. I was never prone to headaches before. They started before I'd finished taking the pills. They just came – boom. We rang the doctor and he said, 'Oh yes, that happens. Go and get some Mersyndol [a painkiller].' It did help a bit. I had a massive headache for a couple of months. I walked the house, I walked the bike track. I got a special ice-pack. I wanted to die so many times. The reason I'm still alive is that I don't want to leave my children with guilt. I've had a headache for two and a half years. The headache will move around. Normally it's either at the back of my skull, which is always painful, or it's deep in my forehead.

Then there is a feeling that my brain has been exposed and somebody has dunked it in hot water, because I get these awful hot flushes in my head, and I feel as if someone has scraped their nails over my exposed brain, and it's bloody sore. When I have a really bad day I take some Mersyndol and that helps to put me to sleep.

I complain all the time that somebody is inside my head and they have a vice which they keep tightening. Even as I'm speaking to you now my brain is actually jumping. People are walking around in gumboots. At other times my head is just full of so much pressure that I want to open a door and let some steam out. The only way I can let that steam out is really, really cry. There is something going on in my head all the time – it's never giving me any peace.

My depression was connected with the headaches. It was abominable up to the last three months. Before that it was with me without let-up – I couldn't see any hope for life. Even with my new grandchildren I couldn't see anything to live for. There was nothing. It was the blackest black room, and I used to cry to my counsellor, 'I'm in this black room.' He used to tell me to walk across the room and raise the blind. I'd say, 'But there is no blind.' He'd say, 'Draw one, make one on the wall and then pull it up.' It was so dark, so black, and it would go on for weeks. All I can remember is walking, and even when I walked I took the black room with me. I couldn't see the trees, I couldn't see the flowers.

I took Sinequan, an anti-depressant, for several months. I had to or I'd have died of the depression. We're talking suicidal thoughts here, we're talking despair. I'd wake up every morning and think, oh no, I can't go on. I couldn't get out of bed. My counsellor said, 'Get out of bed, draw a door, draw a window and crawl through it.' It went on for so many months. I'd walk three or four hours and I'd have no memory of it. I found it hard to come inside the house; somehow it seemed to be darker.

I always seem to be shaking. I feel as if I'm quite still but everything is rattling around inside, like a

school case or a pencil case with everything rattling around. That's what my insides do. There
doesn't seem to be any end to these symptoms.
I've got hot flushes, like menopause all over again. It
comes and goes. My hair is actually wet. My
daughter took my temperature during one of
these spells and it was normal.

Just of late I've begun to think it's a blessing
that I'm no longer sleeping with my husband
because I know that I am fluffing during the night
and it's uncontrollable. Not that I can sleep
anyway although it's not as bad as it was. I was a fab-
ulous sleeper; my husband used to say that I was the
only person he knew who could go to sleep on the
way to bed.

I still have very bad nightmares. All sorts of
thoughts and feelings that I don't want will come
into my head. I envisage dangers the whole time,
usually to my grandchildren. If I hear on the news
that there is a child down a drain it immediately
becomes one of my grandchildren. I can be driving along and suddenly I'll begin to imagine my
daughter in the car with her children and they
have all been decapitated. Imagining my family in
danger, never myself. I'd walk down by the creek and
if it had been raining and the creek was flowing
my grandchildren were in there, and I'd imagine
myself jumping in. So real; I could see their little
heads bobbing about in the current.

I'd get on the phone and ring my daughter, or
I'd ring Lifeline and talk to some inexperienced
person who would say, what are you afraid of, and
I'd say, I'm just afraid. I'd be whispering into the
phone so my husband wouldn't hear me. My first

thought every day was, it's not real, this is not happening to me. Then I'd become fully conscious and realise I had to face another fifteen hours of this pain.

I was tormented at home, but going out was even worse. When I first came off the pills, during that first week, I went into town on the train and I couldn't come home. The train trip was dreadful – I got off at every third station. There were windows in the old trains, but in the new ones the guard closes the doors and you can't open the windows. I'm fine with public transport now.

I couldn't go into supermarkets. I used to give a note to one of the checkout girls. I hated driving. Traffic lights were my problem – I couldn't stop at the stoplights. I felt trapped – I just wanted to get out and scream. I did do that. I was coming back from my daughter's and I stopped – it was getting dark. I was on the righthand side and there were two other rows of traffic on my left. I just stopped the car, got out on to the traffic island and screamed my head off.

When all the other cars had gone I dangerously drove to the side of the road, went to a side street, jumped out of the car, and ran up and down the street sobbing into my beloved old tweed over-coat. It took me about three hours to get from there to home. I drove home slowing down at all the red lights, and after that I didn't get in a car for two years. I couldn't even be a passenger in a car for a long time.

All these symptoms come and go erratically. But there has been some improvement. The fact that I can drive the car again is an improvement. I have a burst of activity and then I get tired. My extraordinary unknown fears seem to have subsided – I still get them but not nearly so often. The intensity of my panic attacks is much, much lower – I can get a bit panicky but I can talk myself out of it. For example two weeks ago I had a medical test which involved being strapped down for an hour. A year ago I could never have done this.

The whole thing varies so much. Last week I'd have said I'm well on the way heading down the straight. This week I'm just leaving the post. The last fortnight I'd give myself a nine out of ten for extreme pain; now it's down to two or three. Before this last fortnight I was about seven out of ten and ready to climb Mt Everest. If I didn't have the headaches I could cope with the little bit of anxiety I get. But I still can't cope with stress.

I find that meditation helps with that. I've always been a meditator but I've never been able to meditate as strongly as I could before benzos, but I persist. I would recommend it without reservation – and group meditation is even better. I'd say, get someone to teach you to meditate. No reflexology – it stirs up all the nerves in the brain and it made me really ill. Gentle massage only.

Common sense tells me all these symptoms are withdrawal, but then when my head gets really bad I am positive I have a brain tumour. I've had a brain scan which showed there is no pathology in my head, but even then I doubted it. Only in hindsight can I be really sure that it was withdrawal.

I'm positive that all these symptoms are benzo-related, but I am still afraid.

RUTH
Disintegration of an artist

*Ruth, in her forties, is an artist and sculptor. She
started taking Valium in the mid-1970s and it is six
years since she took her last benzodiazepine. She is
one of many people for whom the first prescription
led to other mind-altering drugs, at the very worst
stage of her addiction.*

*Benzodiazepines are the one constant thread
right through her unhappy story. Ruth is convinced
that they were the root of her problem.*

*Her withdrawal from benzos has been extremely
severe and intense. One of the worst things was that
she lost her creativity, but this has now returned and
Ruth has done some compelling drawings depicting
her experiences on benzos. Now almost recovered,
she is doing a course and preparing for an
exhibition of her work.*

Before I was put on benzodiazepines, I had never
had any serious illness in my whole life. I very
rarely got a virus and I was always full of energy. I
never thought about being healthy – I was healthy.

In about 1976 I got a bout of pleurisy which was
causing muscle cramping and I was prescribed

Valium, a muscle relaxant. I was never told any-thing about it. I never, ever went to the doctor and said I was feeling nervous. Before the tablets I was sleeping well, but over a period of time my story is of the disintegration of a human being.

In 1977 I was working very hard. I got an exhibi-tion going and I was beginning to sell work. I had a number of mixed exhibitions after a one-woman exhibition. I was slowly beginning to sell and gain a reputation but it just faded out. People would say, 'Are you going to have another exhibition?' And I would say, 'Oh yeah, maybe . . .'

Everything was an effort but I didn't want to think about it. I also remember when I was having that first exhibition, someone said, 'Why don't you take Valium? They're tranquillisers.' And I thought, that's funny, they've never made me feel calm.

In 1982 I decided to halve the dose – and I became chronically ill. Looking back I now realise I was in a state of withdrawal for the next six years. I had so many symptoms during that period.

I developed extreme difficulty in breathing and I felt as though I'd become an asthmatic. The chest infection that I was given the Valium for never cleared up completely for all the years I was on the pills, but completely cleared up in 1988 when I came off them. I was in severe pain for years and years with that pleurisy-like chest infection. I had ter-rible thumping headaches. I lost my appetite and when I did eat I often vomited and my weight went down to about seven stone, but in the last few years I was on the pills it ballooned out to four-teen stone. I looked bloated and yellow.

I had chronic diarrhoea all the time I was on the pills. I felt like I had a continual urinary tract infection and would pass water frequently. I had chronic ear problems and was diagnosed as having Ménière's disease because of a loss of balance and nausea. And chronic sinus problems.

I would get spontaneous bruising. I would find little bruises on parts of my body, like the insides of my legs, which could not have been caused by bumping myself. There were awful aches and pains in the muscles and joints, too. I developed, at times, almost a stutter. I felt that words would become blocked when I tried to talk.

I became so agoraphobic that I couldn't go out, but I couldn't stay inside. I think for years on end I was in a state of panic attack – a chronic total panic attack. I noticed a strange smell about me. I was so spaced out, and at times I felt I was almost having visions. I felt I was 'tripping'. I became severely depressed. I attempted suicide at least three times, by taking large amounts of Valium as well as trying to get extra sleeping tablets at the chemist. I was rushed to hospital a couple of times.

I also had outbursts of manic-type hysteria and violent rage. I would smash up everything in my room or destroy my work. At one time I even planned to kill someone. I went from being able to work at my sculptures for sometimes ten to twelve hours a day to being able to do virtually nothing at all. I had so little energy that I thought to myself, just before coming off my tablets, that I didn't have very long to live – maybe a couple of years at the most. I had accepted that this was life –

this was how it was for me as I had spent years lying in bed or on a couch for a lot of the day.

During the benzo years my sexuality was totally destroyed – I sort of felt like a thing. I felt so physically and mentally ill. My sex drive would fluctuate from not being there at all to feeling uncontrollably 'turned on'. But I could never get any satisfaction. I felt like some sort of sex maniac.

I developed severe PMT and extremely heavy periods. The PMT included very bad fluid retention and irritability, even worse depression and severe migraines.

There were bad sleep disturbances which led me to taking extra tablets at night. I had frequent nightmares and severe night sweats – I would have to change my clothes in the middle of the night. I needed at least twelve hours' sleep and often stayed in bed until the afternoon.

I became mentally ill. At one stage my personality had disintegrated so much that I became obsessed with stealing from shops. In my mind, shoplifting became necessary for my sanity. Each day when I got up I would prepare for the day's shoplifting. I would sort of psych myself up. Every day I would go into shops and stuff all sorts of things down my jeans, under my coat, in my pockets and under my arms. I also worked out that if you were standing at a counter and you focused your eyes on the person serving you and talked to them, you could go along the counter and pinch everything from under their eyes.

Eventually I got caught trying to stuff a large bag of kitty litter under my coat. Apparently the shop detective was watching me do this. I got out through the turnstile and it fell out. I was charged with shoplifting and taken to the police station. The police, who were very nice to me, gave me a feed of Kentucky Fried Chicken because they thought I was so thin.

I started identifying with the homeless street people in St Kilda, and thought, this is where I really belong, on the edge of society.

All this occurred when I was taking my highest doses of benzos. My life was totally destroyed and I never at any stage had any idea that the state I had got into was because of the drugs. I had been given large amounts of antibiotics to cure the chest infection, which they never did. I was pre-scribed major tranquillisers and anti-depressants for a while. I was drinking alcohol heavily, every day.

For some reason, I couldn't get enough ciga-rettes and I was buying sleeping tablets from the chemist. And sometimes I was on Lomotil anti-diarrhoea tablets. It was at this time that I attempted suicide at least three times.

I had lost my ability to think, so it was impossible to reason things out or draw conclusions and make associations. I just knew that I had become a severely mentally and physically ill person, with-out hope. This was always reinforced by doctors who were telling me that I needed to be on the tablets, perhaps for the rest of my life.

No doctor ever mentioned side-effects or said that the benzos were extremely addictive. Only my present doctor in 1988 mentioned that I was addicted to them. I was also sent to several psy-chiatrists and psychologists who screwed me up even more because the symptoms I was talking about – depression, the shoplifting – were actually due to benzos.

At the beginning of 1988 I happened to go back to a doctor I used to see years ago. I went there because I was not happy with my current psychologist and I thought he might know a better one. This doctor was becoming aware of the problems caused by benzos. He told me I was addicted to them and sent me to a tranquilliser support group.

A person at that group sat me down and said, 'You are in this state because of the tablets.' She said that many of the symptoms I had mentioned were common in benzo withdrawal. I went home and started to reduce my tablets. I never put up any fight – I just started to reduce them. I had already halved the dose in 1982 but I was still on three or four Valium a day.

I had to go back to my local doctor at one stage that year because I was so ill I couldn't get to the doctor I was seeing. I told her I was going to a tranquilliser support group and she sneered at me and shook her head. She did not believe there was any withdrawal.

It took me nearly the whole year to come off the Valium as I was so ill. I had dreadful paranoia and bizarre thoughts.

I had awful hallucinations. A feeling of unreality and horrible detachment. It felt like I was in some other dimension. One time I remember looking into the mirror and not knowing what side I was on.

In withdrawal I had the most terrible sexual fantasies and obsessions that were only just under control. I had them about total strangers in the street – I would stare at people and if they became aware of me staring at them I would find ways to watch them without them becoming aware of it – like if I was in a train and staring at them, I would suddenly look in the window and see if I could see them, so I could have a good perve. Male or female, it didn't matter which. When the obsession went I would look at the person concerned and think, what was I doing? I had sexual fantasies about men, women, children, animals. Sometimes I would be so turned on by someone, for instance someone serving in a shop, that I would stop going there because I would start shaking.

I would cry about all sorts of things at the drop of a hat. If I was looking at television I would just start sobbing at something which would make someone else feel a bit weepy.

Sometimes one side of my face would go numb with migraines, and the tunnel vision would be more one-sided. It was my right side which was bad. When this first happened I thought I was having a stroke. One time I became convinced that I had changed from being left-handed to right-handed. But I knew that if I'd picked up a pencil, I couldn't have written with my right hand.

I had bad muscle spasms and pains all over my body, particularly in my neck and shoulders, lower back, lower legs and feet. My feet also became swollen. I had bouts of severe pain for about a year after coming off the pills. Much of that has gone but I still have some pain in my neck. At times the pain was so bad in my jaw that one night I seriously considered hitting my head against the wall. That almost completely went away some time ago and I rarely have it now.

I had audio-hallucinations with strange bird-like chattering that went on for months on end. I had extreme sensitivity to sound. I couldn't wear my watch because the ticking was unbearable. I could not listen to music as it would bring on a panic attack. The Ménière's disease disappeared soon after I came off the tablets, after years of having it.

My nose bled repeatedly on the tablets and in withdrawal. I had extreme sensitivity to smell and severe sinus pain – on the tablets and through the worst of withdrawal. These symptoms have now gone. Very occasionally I get a little bit but not often.

For years my face was yellowy-grey and bloated looking. My skin peeled and was oily and I came out in pimples. I had very dark circles under my eyes and my face looked like some strange mask. At the stage when I was still very skinny, I was waiting in the chemist for a prescription and a person nearly tripped over me because she thought I was a shop dummy.

I stopped doing just about everything in withdrawal except the simplest household tasks. I could never have held down even a part-time job during this time. My own artwork became impossible to do for years as the tablets completely destroyed my creativity. Not surprisingly I had lost all my friends by then.

I came back to live with my parents in 1985. I was always fairly open with them. I told them how ill

I was and they could see I was no longer able to care for myself. At times if I didn't mention what I was feeling, it was only because I thought it would be too much for them. I didn't want to freak them out. They are both around seventy years of age. They have looked after me all through this illness but it has been very unfair on them. I have my own TV and music and I stay in my room a lot, away from them, to give us both some privacy. I draw and read and leave them to their friends.

I am now two and a half years off medication. I am not fully recovered yet, as there is still a lot that I am not able to cope with. I still have trouble with fatigue. Compared to how I was on the tablets I am much better. There are many symptoms that I don't get any more, which I had for years and years. I can do so many things now. I am enjoying cooking and at times I can draw – not all the time though, as I haven't the energy.

I am now able to think most of the time and concentrate a lot better. The rages that I used to have are no longer there and I am getting my self-esteem back. I no longer have the terrible despair as so many things are improving all the time – slowly, but they are happening. Virtually all the phobias that became a part of my life over the years have gone. My creative drive is coming back too. I have a sense of hope for my life except for when I think of how long this process is taking.

I still get some low-key anxiety and I couldn't cope with the stress of a relationship yet. Those big feelings that you get – I'm not up to that yet – I have to keep on an even keel. I still have to take things very easily. I can do far more activities than

I've been able to do since I've been on the tablets, but I have to take rests during the day, otherwise I get that strange light-headedness. I get slight weepy feelings if I push myself – I get agitated. I feel fragile.

I am on an invalid pension and when I am well enough to work I will not need any encouragement because I am very keen to get on with my life. On a scale of one to ten, I place myself at six and a half. I feel that, in time, I will recover completely. I'll be stronger physically, mentally and emotionally – and more creative.

I am still amazed that I got through this journey to where I am today. I know that most people never have to find in themselves what we are all called on to find in withdrawal.

If I had known what these tablets were going to do to me I would never have gone near them in a fit. What makes me very angry is that in my younger days I was sometimes offered drugs like heroin, cocaine, amphetamines and LSD and I always refused to take them, because I didn't want anything to interfere with my creativity. Then I happened to go to the doctor and I was given a drug which is worse than all of them. It totally destroyed my life in every way – relationships, health and sanity. I think benzodiazepines are an obscenity against life in its deepest meaning.

MADELEINE
Singer out of tune

Madeleine, in her late forties, is a well-known and successful opera singer who has performed in Europe and the USA. She was first prescribed benzos for stress symptoms that she suspects may actually have been caused by some chemicals she was using in her home. She took the pills for one year – eight months of which were spent coming off very slowly. Although she was only on a small dose, she found they were causing severe problems after only four months. Madeleine had no protracted withdrawal period; in fact, she recovered as soon as she stopped taking benzos.

About two years ago I woke in the middle of the night with my heart going boom, boom, boom. I thought I was having a heart attack or something. My husband called an ambulance which took me to the hospital. I had everything checked out and they couldn't find anything odd.

I thought maybe stress was causing the heart problem. I went to my local doctor and he suggested Valium. I wasn't even drinking coffee or tea, so I was wary. I knew of Valium and I said, 'No,

I'm not going on that!' But I was feeling really uptight and really high-strung, so he said, 'What about minor tranquillisers?' Now, minor means minor to me – less – so I thought they would be all right to try. I was given Murelax.

After two weeks I finished the first prescription. I was at home and I said to my husband, 'James, I think I have to go to the doctor, I think I'm dying, the heart is starting to go again!' So he took me down to the doctor, and there was a full waiting room but I said to the receptionist, 'Look, I don't think I can wait, I'm really bad.' The doctor saw me and took out some more tablets and told me to take one. Both he and I thought the problem was my stress.

I took them for one year continuously. They were helpful for four weeks. Then I suddenly realised I was taking the maximum dose, four a day. I took one, say, every six hours. The first two hours I didn't feel anything. Hour three and four it was very helpful because then I was as 'normal'. I wasn't thinking about taking the next tablet. By the fifth hour I was starting to think, when can I take the next one? By the sixth hour I was really counting the minutes.

In the last hour before I was due to take another tablet I would have symptoms. I would feel them coming on and know I needed to take another tablet. I know these effects would have gotten even worse if I'd stopped the tablets dead.

The anxiety was the big thing. With it I would get panic attacks, and there was no reason for this panic. I would get pain and palpitations. Despair. Fear. I had never had anxiety like this before. I was born placid, so I'm not used to being nervous, worrying, depressed. Before a performance it is usual to have heart-dread, but you don't get panic, you don't think you're going to die.

I would get a feeling like an electric shock between the ears – Boing!

I've never depended on anything, and I suddenly realised I couldn't go out of the house without a tablet in my pocket. I would wake up at four o'clock every night and take the tablet.

First I tried to talk to people for help. The family doctor said, 'No, you need this medication now, you're under terrible stress.' I spoke to my best friend who used to be the chemist in the village who said, 'Don't worry about it; I don't know how many people I provide them for. If you need it, you need it, people take it for years.'

After the first four weeks, I got so angry. I lived with anger for ten months. I'm a loner, I don't like communicating with people, but this anger made me speak at a ladies lunch about my dependence. Seven of the twenty present either were depending or had people in their family depending.

I realised no one was taking me seriously, and I didn't know where to go for help. I contacted AA. Finally in the paper I read about a local drug agency. They put me on to a meditation group, and that's what saved me. I also started to meditate.

Four months after I first took Murelax I started to come off them, very, very slowly. Within two months I had cut down to two tablets by myself, just by meditating. But I was not able to cut down the last two by myself. I would get panic, and I thought, I will get an attack and I'll die. I was very worried when I had to perform at the Opera House after cutting down to only two tablets. But it went fine, and that gave me confidence.

The next month I had to go to Sweden. I could speak my own language there and maybe explain in more detail my situation. I wanted to find somewhere where they could 'just take care of me' while I came off those last two tablets, even if I was going to get hallucinations.

I saw a doctor who was shocked that I had been on four a day. She recommended against hospitalisation, and suggested I continue myself, but much more slowly. So I started then to cut down by an eighth at a time. I was able to do it this way with no ill-effects. The whole reduction took about eight months.

I might have felt panicky five times since coming off the pills eighteen months ago. Through meditation I've been able to handle it straight away. If I hadn't been able to meditate, maybe it would have been worse.

What worried me most was that I didn't have information. I was faced with something I had no knowledge about, that I'd never experienced before in my life. And people didn't know, didn't want to tell you, or they rubbished it.

Funnily enough it's as if I lost that whole year of my life. I was not functioning normally because I was totally depending on the tablets. It's not you controlling situations – these things are controlling you.

I now consider myself to be completely recovered.

PAULA
Mother's vigil keeps her awake

*Paula is a resilient woman in her early fifties who
has had one tragedy too many in her life. In the end
she started taking sleeping pills. For five years they
became a habit she could not break. Paula had her
worst symptoms while she was still taking benzos.
After four or five months she was over the worst of
her withdrawal, and was completely recovered
within a year.*

I started to take sleeping pills – Mogadons –
because of stress, family problems. Our son was
very ill and we were told he might die. I wasn't
sleeping very well and it seemed to me that they
were a great help at the time. At the same time as
our son was so ill, we lost our parents – my dad and
both my husband's parents. The doctor empha-
sised that we must get a good night's sleep. We
had already lost two children earlier in our marriage. You probably get enough sleep from
exhaustion in the end.

The doctor had prescribed Serepax for my husband, but he hadn't taken them – they made him feel
terrible. I took one each night for six nights, and

they made me feel very bloated. I kept looking at myself and thinking, I'm out of it. I felt very panicky then, because I felt so strange. I was frightened for no reason – very scared. I had nightmares too. The feelings didn't last long but they were very intense. I think I would have ended up in hospital if I'd continued taking them, as the side-effects were so severe. I thought that I would never touch Serepax again but my doctor convinced me that Mogadons were much, much different. I thought that he must know.

They did help me get to sleep for a couple of years, but I kept taking them for about five years. I started out taking half a tablet when I needed it for about two years, and then continuously one a night.

I really seemed to be much worse while I was on the pills. I didn't know what was wrong with me, I just thought I was stressed and ill. I was so paranoid then and always crying. I used to get anxious and very depressed, even when things were going well. I was quite despairing at times. There are so many people who are worse off than you and you think, why am I so depressed?

Once I felt like killing myself, so I had to call the minister. I was going to take an overdose. I couldn't explain why I wanted to kill myself – I just thought nobody loved me and they didn't need me. It was terrible. I even put paper in the typewriter – I was going to write to my husband, my son and daughter – just explain that I loved them but I couldn't go on.

I don't understand why I should have had such bad suicidal thoughts then, because there have been many other times when things have been much worse, such as when we were told our son wouldn't live. I felt strong then – I had to keep going. You hope it never happens again. Then I think I could never do that to my family – leave behind that heartache.

On the pills I used to wake up feeling tired, although I'd had a good night's sleep. It wasn't a natural sleep, so I wasn't surprised. I used to get lots of small bruises and they worried me. They tested me for leukaemia because I got them for so long – years. I had bad headaches, but as soon as I came off benzos they went away. My muscles aren't sore now like they were then and neither are my breasts – they were really sore. My stomach was tied up in knots. Sometimes I felt I was more uptight in the daytime than I was before I started taking the Mogadon.

I felt I was getting too dependent on the pills, but decided that I would keep taking them and hope that one day I would be able to go off them – perhaps when my son died or I got over all my problems, but it doesn't work that way really. I had tried to go off pills when we went on holidays but I couldn't sleep. Another reason I wanted to stop taking them was because my husband wasn't happy about me being on them. He saw me taking one sometimes and said that I had better cut them out. I felt I should listen to him.

I thought that they had definitely become a habit, no matter what the doctor said. Every time he prescribed the tablets, I would say that I was worried about becoming hooked on them, and he would say, you're not hooked, you just need them. He was the one who talked me into taking them in the first place, saying, you're stressed, you're stressed – you should be on them, you need something to help you sleep.

I was really concerned that I would never be able to stop taking them. So I stopped, cold turkey. I threw out my repeat prescription and I thought, this is it. I wasn't afraid to come off them because I didn't expect to have any serious side-effects. I expected to have sleepless nights for a while, even though the doctor said I wouldn't. But I didn't tell him until later, when I said I'd gone off Mogadons cold turkey. He said that he supposed that was good.

I've been off the pills for about a year. I could never swallow one again.

I think that the only symptom which was worse when I came off was my stomach pain and discomfort. It got much worse, and I had to have a gastroscopy. But they didn't find anything wrong at all. I had bad nightmares for the first three nights, and I felt that the bed was tipping up. That went on for about three weeks. It frightened me. I didn't sleep well for quite a while. I'm much better now – I only wake up once during the night, and I get about seven or eight hours' sleep. The real difference is that I wake up feeling like I have been to sleep.

I still got anxious and depressed for a while after I came off. In fact I thought about suicide again. But I found that having someone to talk to helped a bit. I could talk to my husband although I wasn't completely truthful with him. I must have been ashamed of taking pills – I didn't tell anyone else. I thought I should have been able to cope without them – that I should have been able to sleep and not worry at night.

It was only this morning that I realised that I hadn't told my best friend, and I share so much with her. She knows about my stomach problems. I am open about a lot of things. I tell her about my concerns when my son is having his hospital tests, and what will happen to him. But I have never told her this. I must have been ashamed – thought that I should have been depending on God more instead of giving in to tablets. I come from a very anti-tablet family.

I am fully recovered now. It took longer than I thought it would, quite a few months. I now think that I had problems that I didn't connect with withdrawing from Mogadon.

My nextdoor neighbour has so many tranquillisers that he is always offering some to me. He has retired and is on thirteen different tablets – he has been on them for years. He always looks dreamy and has a rest in the daytime.

TOM
Blood-boiling rage

*Tom is in his late thirties. He was first prescribed
benzodiazepines in 1973 while he was still at university. He was living the life of a typical young stu-
dent: parties, drinking, smoking a bit of dope,
driving taxis at night, jogging to try to make up for it.
This fast-lane lifestyle led to a couple of 'funny turns'
or panic attacks – and to his first Valium script.
Later he married and became a teacher, but he was
still on Valium. He took it for thirteen years.*

*Tom had a very intense withdrawal experience.
He suffered severe lethargy and depression, and
from being a peaceful person he became violent
and aggressive. But in the end he made a very
strong recovery and feels his life is now even better
than it was before.*

After I'd been on Valium for about two years I
decided to stop taking them. I'd been off them for a
month when I suddenly had a panic attack on the
freeway driving back from the airport. It just got
worse and worse. This reaction was far more
severe than my original problem. In hindsight I
realise that out of the blue withdrawal decided to hit

149

me. I couldn't handle the symptoms on my own, so I went back on a higher dose of the pills. I started taking them whenever I needed them, sometimes eight per day.

Over the next few years I developed all sorts of ailments which no one could ever explain – in my chest, my gut, my lungs. I couldn't do aerobic exercise any more. I used to think it was just me panicking, but now I understand that it was a real physical thing: I couldn't get enough air into my lungs.

I lost three stone – I was getting into jeans I now couldn't get my left leg into. I had developed agoraphobia about a month after I first started taking the pills. I didn't even know what it was at the time – someone had to tell me.

The dentist told me my teeth were breaking down. He'd find fifteen fillings to do over six months. Then I'd go six months later and there'd be five more. I went back after I'd come off Valium because I had a filling that had washed out. He said I had very strong teeth, and should not have all those fillings. From having the worst teeth in the world I suddenly had the best. I think they came back strongly after withdrawal, like a boost of energy, as though the body had rushed to their aid.

I knew I was physically addicted to Valium but I never wanted to take the rotten things. I used to pick them up in the morning and think, you bastards, you've really got a hold on me. I hated the fact that I needed them, but I accepted it too. If I didn't take them I couldn't avoid the symptoms, but I didn't twig that they were causing the symptoms I was trying to avoid.

Then one day my wife found an article in the newspaper. She never reads the paper at work, but on that day she did. She gets to page 21 and here's this full-page article on benzodiazepines: 'If you feel the following things . . . you are addicted to tranquillisers.' She brought it home and said, 'Read that.' I said, 'Yeah yeah, another bloody article about what I've got to do now, another psychological treatise for me to enjoy.'

I did read the article – and I swore someone had been tracing my life history. It was pinpointing everything I'd complained about for twelve years. The penny dropped straight away – it was like Zen enlightenment: bang! Oh no! You idiot, you dickhead, why didn't you see this? I couldn't see the most obvious thing. I always thought the only thing between me and physical and mental insanity was my Valium. They were the one thing I had to cling to.

But I was frightened shitless of coming off those pills. Having experienced the early stages of withdrawal, I knew that you are into uncharted waters, so I decided to put myself into hospital. Even there it was all still very experimental and I was drifting into the unknown. What is going to happen to me next? How bizarre is it going to be? Frightening – so severe! The strength of these symptoms is enormous.

The alcoholics in the hospital got better in ten days. They would come off the grog, start eating again, and they'd bloom. They'd be saying, what's wrong with you, you've been in here longer than us? We'd have hair hanging down, grey faces, getting worse not better.

My reduction took six weeks. I stayed nine and a half weeks in hospital because I was violently depressed. I took Sinequan [an anti-depressant] for about six months to help me with this. I started those about a fortnight after I came off Valium, and they probably saved me. I was very negative, and they picked up my attitude almost overnight. I remember waking up starving hungry, and really looking forward to getting going. It was a turning point for my recovery. I had no trouble coming off the Sinequan – I reduced the dosage slowly over about a month and had no ill-effects.

I am now five and a half years off the pills. I don't think anyone even at my stage of recovery can accurately convey the extreme mental, emotional and physical pain that you can suffer in the withdrawal process. No one who hasn't been through it can have an inkling of what it's like.

One of the greatest problems I had in withdrawal was a raging temper. I've heard experts call it 'irritability'. In fact it was a blood-boiling rage which took me all my time to manage. I used to thump doors, walls, furniture – anything to express it. I'd swear uncontrollably, kick and bash anything until the anger went away.

My wife was the butt of my verbal outbursts. I'd call her all the names under the sun. I accused her of infidelity – stupidity – theft – ugliness – anything that came to mind. How she took it and continued to live with me I'll never know. I picked on certain people all the time, especially my mother-in-law. I shouted and abused them – I was never happy till my victim was in tears. While I was doing this I couldn't be convinced that my anger was not logical

– it seemed so real. I don't have this problem any longer, and now I can see how terrible it must have been for everyone who was close to me.

As well as this I had morbid thoughts. Mental images of tombstones – of my own rotting flesh – and I'd see myself lying in a grave. These thoughts often became obsessive. They were black, morose, ugly, and in my mind I couldn't escape the horror. I'd sit staring for ages, trying to regain control over my mind. Then the thoughts would just suddenly click off without any effort from me.

I was overwhelmingly anxious in the mornings for absolutely no reason. My body shook, tightened, sweated, heaved – so badly I really thought I was going to die. Panic attacks to me were a crazy heightened fear and an overwhelming sense that I was going to die. A lion jumps out of the bush at you. It was definitely a physical thing and left you drained afterwards. They only lasted thirty seconds, but God . . .

Lethargy and fatigue – unbelievable! I felt like a zombie. I'm sure I looked like one. The tiredness you earn from when you've done something energetic is a good feeling. But this is like a plague. It was waking up and feeling that you needed a good night's sleep – or the strain of picking a book up off the floor. One time I went to the clothes line to bring in a few things, and had to sit down on the lawn for a while because I was too bloody exhausted to walk back to the house! You really weren't exhausted; your body was just feeling that way as a result of withdrawal. It comes on more during periods of stress. In the early days it was accompanied by depression which creates fatigue.

My forearms felt like I had RSI. I could hardly write. Sometimes I could hardly dress myself. Once when I was about two and a half years off I woke up and I couldn't move my neck. I was in extreme pain. We'd been away for two weeks. It was a spasm that the physio put down to sleeping on different pillows during the holiday. Then I realised, bugger that, this is withdrawal. It came out of the blue and just vanished and has never come back.

My bowels were badly affected. I used to say to my wife, 'It feels like my bowel is searching for tomorrow morning's breakfast.' I couldn't leave the toilet I was in so much pain because every time I got up I had to go back, and sure enough I'd have to go back in again. Someone said to me at a support group meeting that the amount that he did in the toilet far exceeded his capacity to eat. I couldn't eat that much in a week. I had a terrible ache in my bum and thighs, rumbling and a real screamy noise. I ended up with severe haemorrhoids from the strain.

I could never bring the washing in because I couldn't tell whether things were dry or not. If I tested the heat of the water I had to put the back of my hands in – not my fingers. There was lack of feeling, yet if I got a tiny little scratch on my finger or if a hair touched it, I knew.

I also had that funny feeling that there is an earthquake happening. I used to stand there and think, don't notice me anyone. That came and went until last year sometime. Early on I had dizziness like I was doing an elliptical orbit in my head. I had disorientation as to direction twice – came out of a shop and didn't know which way was which, and felt really frightened.

Originally when I was first coming off, there was a feeling of shuddering inside – it was as though someone was patting me on the back or the chest and me moving, but it never came outside the body, it was always in here somewhere. It was like someone pushing something from the inner to the outer edge of my body but it never came out. I grew a beard for the first four months so I didn't have to shave.

The most insane problem was the feeling of unreality – that I wasn't here, that I didn't exist. I can't describe this properly. For what seemed like ages I'd feel like I had no being. I'd ask people to tell me I was still here. That caused a lot of problems, especially with people who didn't believe in withdrawal. Try telling someone you feel as if you're not here.

For the life of me I don't know how I survived all this. There were times when the symptoms were so intense that it didn't seem to matter whether I lived or died. It all seemed so useless and crazy, and the joke was on me. No one gets better when they're as close to death as I felt I was. There were times when it was only the lack of a gun that stopped me from doing myself in.

But it was just that depth of agony that gave me the strength to continue. My mind and body tried to convince me that I would never get better, but it wasn't true. My symptoms got better slowly and gradually. I just crawled along like a turtle with occasional erratic symptoms. Now the fear is gone. So is the anxiety, the agoraphobia. I feel like I am part of this world again.

I didn't work for twelve months, didn't socialise for three – and even then with great difficulty. We had to put off having any children until I was reasonably well out of it. It all came together after about eighteen months and we were able to start making plans for the future. Up until then I just lived from day to day.

I can do most things these days but I steer away from stress. I just can't imagine the last five years taken up with pill-popping. It would have restricted everything we've done. My life has flourished in the last five years compared to what it was. I've done things that wouldn't have been possible on the pills, such as moving to the country – I was clinging to the dirty old city.

Positive things are family life, children, stronger marriage, greater financial security. My self-esteem is very high – and why not? I have overcome a great problem. I have proved my strength, character, determination. I feel I have a greater degree of psychological stability than many people could hope to reach. I now have a strength I didn't have before that enables me to rise to the occasion, whatever comes along.

Part III

....

An A–Z of
Benzo Symptoms

This section contains an alphabetical list of descriptions of the physical, mental and emotional symptoms reported by people who have gone through benzodiazepine withdrawal. Some may have only a few, while others might experience nearly all of the symptoms at one time or another. They can occur while people are still taking their pills, when they are coming off, and after they have stopped altogether.

Benzo withdrawal is erratic. The severity of the symptoms varies, and they are often random and unpredictable: people may feel well for a few days then be plunged into sickness, or they may feel fine before lunch and sick in the afternoon. There is no logical explanation for this, although stress and fatigue do seem to play a part.

The pattern of recovery over a longer period is also unpredictable. For some people it takes a few weeks or months to recover; for others it may be years before they feel completely well again. A small number are fine for a few weeks after they come off their pills, and then withdrawal symptoms strike. It is not uncommon for bouts of withdrawal to return after people believe they are substantially recovered.

It is important to consult your doctor if you are not sure about symptoms. For example, heart irregularities, breast lumps or any unusual bleeding should always be checked.

A–Z OF BENZO SYMPTOMS

Agoraphobia and
claustrophobia
Anger
Anxiety and fear
Appetite and weight
Bladder
Body odour
Bowels
Breathing and lungs
Breasts
Bruising
Concentration and
metal sharpness
Confidence
Crying jags
Decision-making and
judgement
Depression and suicidal
thoughts
Dexterity and motor co-
ordination
Dizziness
Dreams and nightmares
Eyes and vision
Face and appearance
Fatigue and lethargy
Flu-like symptoms
Genitals
Hair
Head
Hearing
Heart and pulse

Jaw
Left/Right-sided
symptoms
Manic episodes and
mood swings
Memory
Menstruation
Motivation and
enthusiasm
Mouth and tongue
Muscles and joints
Numbness/pins and
needles
Panic attacks
Paranoia
Phobias
Restlessness and
agitation
Secretions
Sexuality
Shaking and inner
tremor
Skin
Sleep problems
Social and
communication
skills
Stomach
Strange sensations and
electric shocks
Sweating and body
temperature

Taste	Unreality and
Teeth and gums	depersonalisation
Throat	Voice and speech

AGORAPHOBIA AND CLAUSTROPHOBIA

Agoraphobia is defined as 'a morbid fear of open spaces and public places', and claustrophobia as 'a morbid fear of confined places'. These may seem to be complete opposites, but in benzo withdrawal they often overlap or even happen simultaneously: 'I couldn't leave my room because of the agoraphobia but I also had to have the window wide open because of the claustrophobia – I would feel that I was suffocating.'

These conditions, which seem to affect almost all sufferers, share very similar symptoms: overwhelming fear, dizziness and loss of balance, jelly legs, sweating, disorientation, panic attacks and palpitations. They can start very soon after benzos are first prescribed, and are one of the first signs that addiction is developing. Often people have never heard of agoraphobia before.

> I was so agoraphobic that at my worst I found it impossible to leave my room, and sometimes my bed. When I did try to go out into the backyard, my legs wouldn't take my weight and I would feel like vomiting.

> Agoraphobia was one of my first reactions to taking the pills. I got it about six months after I started on Valium. I'd be walking round in town and 'it' would creep over me. I would feel

hideously out of control, anxious, with a wafty disconnected head. It was a nauseous, damp, sweaty
feeling. I went to a psychiatrist and he said in an off-
handed fashion, 'Oh, just blow into a paper bag.'

There would be so many occasions when I
would be sitting in restaurants with friends
(having swallowed another half a Valium as I was
going inside) and I would have to go outside for a
walk because I just couldn't sit there any longer.
As soon as I was outside I was all right.

It seems that as soon as you move away the
panic lifts, but as soon as you get into that situation
again it comes back.

The situations that can provoke benzo-related
agoraphobia or claustrophobia are: supermarkets,
large shopping malls, cinemas, theatres, restaurants, hospitals, airports, big sporting events,
hairdressers, banks, automatic teller machines,
queues, public transport and, for some, cars.
These are all public places where sufferers do not
feel safe, or feel they are being watched. People
fear making fools of themselves in public. Crowds
and bright artificial light can also make them feel
nervous.

My mother would ask me to go shopping with her
and she'd dawdle around. I just wanted to hurry
up and get out of the place. I'd be getting into a
real panic attack before I got out of the store. I
couldn't bear to talk to the cashier about the
transaction, I couldn't relax and be myself
because I was in withdrawal.

The train journeys were agonising. I had about twelve stations to travel and I always had to catch a train that stopped at every station. I couldn't stand it if the train was too crowded, but on the other hand I wanted someone in the carriage in case I became seriously ill. Sometimes the anxiety would be so great that I couldn't go from one station to the next; I'd have to get off. And then I'd have to let two or three trains go by before I had the courage to get on again. On the occasions when the train stopped between stations, I don't know how I controlled myself. I just wanted to pass out. I contemplated climbing out the windows or door but I didn't have the energy to drag the door open. The journey was absolute torture . . . In the end I used to walk from the second last station, about three hours every day, so I was draining myself of energy in withdrawal with all this walking in addition to the tortuous ride on the train.

ANGER

'I'm really angry for no reason'

The majority of people often feel very irritable and angry in withdrawal. Angry about what had happened to them and just generally angry for no particular reason. People who have been slow to anger find themselves having to deal with uncontrollable outbursts of rage; others who have quick tempers are terrified they might lose control.

If you sense that I might be angry, you're darned right. Perhaps I should bash a pillow, but that's too mild. My fits of rage just well up inside me for no apparent reason. I've slammed doors, thrown books, sworn and blasphemed like a trooper when what I really wanted to do was pull the pictures off the wall, throw bricks through windows, mutilate myself – I've wanted to demolish my world and tear myself to pieces. The control needed to stay intact is enormous. I hopes it's worth it. At least it saves a repair bill and medical expenses. Perhaps I should see an anger therapist.

'I am frightened by my thoughts'
People are horrified by violent, even homicidal thoughts. They find it hard to talk to others about these thoughts for fear of alienating them.

I was even scared to speak to my doctor about what I was thinking. I thought he might refer me to a psychiatrist, and what then? It didn't bear thinking about. I never had these thoughts before; you hope they will go away but they don't, not until the withdrawal symptoms start to subside. I had them for two years. At least now I never have them – it is as if it was another life. I thought I was going mad. I felt like killing strangers on the bus or people who were talking to me; I wanted to blow their heads off – to see their heads explode, just because I couldn't cope with them.

I used to run through a host of things I'd like to do to people – how to kill them. It freaked me right out; I couldn't have knives lying around my house – my feelings were too violent. I was so scared I would use

them on myself or someone else. Thank God all
that has gone.

'My anger makes me sick'

Too much emotion of any sort in withdrawal
tends to make people ill. Anger is a strong and
particularly draining emotion. Many people found it
was best to avoid any argument or confrontation
during withdrawal.

> I cannot let myself get angry, if I do it brings on
> symptoms – I have to keep on an even keel, in
> calm waters.

> I still have too much anger, and it makes me ill. I still
> don't have my anger sufficiently under control – it is
> too big for me; I can't take rows any more as it
> always precipitates withdrawal symptoms. I know
> this is not the real me as I was always a fairly
> placid person.

ANXIETY AND FEAR

Almost everyone suffers from increased anxiety
in withdrawal. People who take benzos to help
their anxiety find that in the long run it comes
back – only with a greater intensity: 'The word
anxiety just isn't strong enough to communicate
how I felt. One day I sat on a chair for about ten
hours, trembling with a sort of horror.' It is 'free-
floating' anxiety; it comes and goes without any
obvious cause. For the many people who are
given benzos for a life crisis or a physical problem
like back injury, this comes as quite a shock, as

they have never had severe anxiety before.

In amongst the chemically induced anxiety, unresolved issues may emerge from one's earlier life. People may face repressed memories of, for example, abuse or abandonment that surface and cause anxiety. To sort this out may take the help of an expert: 'When I was coming off the pills, I used to go over all the unhappy times I had experienced – taking these drugs made me forget my unhappiness.'

A general feeling of fearfulness may come and go for years – sometimes mild, other times severe. Some people imagine all sorts of horrors which disappear forever after they have got over the worst of withdrawal.

> At first it wasn't anxiety, it was constant terror I felt – I believed everyone does who comes off one of these drugs suddenly. Later, I would be watching television and I would feel this dreadful fear just come over me. Not in response to the television or anything, it was just the after-effects of the drug.

> If something is happening – if I've got people coming, even my daughters coming for lunch, I get anxious. They're coming on Sunday, it's Mothers' Day and they're bringing lunch. They are always asking how they can help. By eleven o'clock on Sunday I'll have a very anxious knot in my gut, which is completely crazy because they're very easy daughters to get along with, and I love them – they're my darlings. It's just that I'm being put on the mat by this anxiety. It's illogical, it's crazy.

Anxiety, oh yes! Before I went on the pills I was the
sort of bloke who would chuck up before playing in
a soccer match. Now, even just going to watch a
soccer match, I'm anxious. I have to force myself to
do everything, even just going for a walk . . . what if
someone walks up to me and says Hi? I live in a
constant state of total anxiety.

APPETITE AND WEIGHT

Weight fluctuation affects many people in benzo
withdrawal, but it is hard to make accurate gener-
alisations as there are so many different stories.
Some lose weight and stay thin; others gain it and
stay fat. One thing they do have in common, however, is that 'it does not feel normal'.

I go on a lot of diets and occasionally fast, but I
actually gain weight. My body doesn't seem to
react to food as it should.

Although individual histories vary so much, the
most frequent pattern is that people become very
thin and anorexic towards the end of their time on
benzos, when they are often very sick indeed.
Appetite disappears; they have to force themselves to eat, and often they go down to well
below their usual body weight. After several
months off pills, normal appetite and enjoyment of
food return, and weight steadily comes back –
often far too much of it.

I got skinnier and skinnier that last year on the
pills – I could circle my thighs with my hands. I

was getting into these tiny little clothes – I've got a few at home still amongst the huge baggy things I'm wearing now. A friend once gasped aloud when she saw me because I was so thin – and it scared the hell out of me. I kept on eating but only with an effort. Food revolted me until about six months off the pills, when my appetite started to come back. From that point I gradually put on weight on until, now, four years down the track, I'm about a stone overweight. I feel like a real porker. I went from anorexic to Miss Piggy within the space of eighteen months.

In some cases loss of appetite is severe.

I thought I would die because I was hardly eating. For twelve months I lived on dry biscuits and lost a stone in weight. My body became so malnourished, I was lethargic and getting yellow in colour. In desperation I went to a dietitian. He told me not to worry, just to eat pizza, fish and chips, anything to put on weight. I was about eight stone on the pills, I lost about a stone and a half when I came off. Now I'm back up to seven but I can't put any more on yet. I have days when I eat really well, then I might go for two days eating virtually nothing.

Food cravings are very common, especially for sugary sweet foods which are very bad for you in withdrawal. There is often an emotional need to eat because eating is so comforting; it calms you and makes you feel safe: 'Because I felt so abnormal, to eat was a normal thing to do.' People often find themselves gorging – pigging out on food as though the body is desperate to replenish itself with lost nutrients: 'I was cooking huge roasts and eating them all myself.'

> If I hadn't been working I would have put on heaps of weight. It was winter when I stopped taking my pills, and I'd have liked to stuff myself with spring rolls, potato cakes, chips and Milky Way bars. Luckily I determined not to succumb to that.

> I've tried several times to go on a diet but I can't; I feel that I need the food. I need to eat because I don't have enough energy. I go through the whole kitchen eating whatever is available. When I try to diet, it is an enormous effort. I feel incredibly hungry, faint, weak, dizzy. I long for food and keep thinking food, food, food all day. I went on a real sugar binge six months off the pills – lollies, cakes, desserts. I was very attracted by cakeshops; I was hanging out for it. Only recently has it died away. It was a real craving; I never craved the pills in that way.

Sometimes food cravings are quite exotic.

> I would look at people's pets or birds in the back yard or swans in the Botanical Gardens and think how I could cook them.

BLADDER

Incontinence, frequency, pain and infections plague almost everyone who is withdrawing from benzos. Sleep is often disturbed by two or three

trips to the toilet. There is often an urgency to
pass water, though some can't pass any urine at
all when they feel they need to, making repeated
trips to the toilet; others have a stinging, burning
feeling.

> Sometimes I would pass so much water that I
> thought I must have kidney failure. It would burn,
> and I had lower back pain with it. I still got little
> bouts of it after two years.

> I was constantly going to the toilet; it was very
> painful, like an abnormal cystitis. It was infuriat-
> ing. For ages I couldn't even go anywhere – as
> soon as I got to the train station I'd have to go to the
> toilet. I still have it and it gets worse just before I
> have my period. It was the first thing I got. It has
> improved – now it just gets painful when I need to
> go. I'd never had any problem before all this hap-
> pened to me.

BODY ODOUR

A strong body odour is quite common, leading
people to change deodorants and bathe more
often – but nothing seems to help. To smell is to be
socially inept or even crude, so it is not surprising
that benzo-induced body odours embarrass
people and strain relationships.

> I never discussed this distasteful symptom with
> anyone – not even my husband. It started some
> time after I was prescribed benzos but it never
> dawned on me that it could be the pills. I wanted to

shower all the time, as my smell disgusted me. My sweat was sticky and the odour was strong, like the smell of footy gear three days after a match.

People also notice that their body odour can change. For some it is a sour smell, for others it's a chemical odour.

It wasn't a normal sweat smell – it was different. I thought I could actually smell the Valium on my clothes and sheets. It was a chemical smell.

BOWELS

Many people find that their bowels seem to go crazy in withdrawal – most commonly with alternating bouts of constipation and diarrhoea, interspersed by wind.

I rarely had a normal bowel motion in those first couple of years. One day it would be rock hard, the next all runny. It didn't seem to matter what I ate. A doctor told me I had all the symptoms of irritable bowel syndrome, but that didn't stop me being terrified it was something worse. I had two investigations of my bowel – both clear.

I had diarrhoea and constipation simultaneously. I'd be constipated for an hour and then I'd have diarrhoea – but I'd still feel constipated.

For some people diarrhoea is by far the worst problem – it can be very severe, leaving them weak, shaky and exhausted. For others the problem is equally severe constipation. Another odd symptom is what one woman described as a 'hyperactive' bowel: 'Some days I can go to the toilet five or six times. It seems like I am getting rid of far more than I have eaten.' Some people also experience a severe anal muscle spasm, which comes on abruptly and lasts ten minutes or more.

> At first everything went straight through me. It's still not what it should be. I have to go first thing every morning, but it's very runny and watery.

> It was hard for me to get around easily because of my diarrhoea – I used to have to get off the train to go to the toilet,

> It felt like a blocked drain, as though my rectum was too small to let it pass through. There was a sensation that I couldn't get it all out – that a lot of stuff was still lurking up there and I had to keep straining to push it out. I ended up with haemorrhoids.

> I had the feeling that my backside was blocked up. It was as if someone had shoved a stick up my bum and I was walking round with it still there. Terrible pain would just come on up my bum. I would sit on the toilet and do my deep breathing, relax, push, do everything I could and after about half an hour it usually went away.

Persistent bad wind is very common – sometimes silent and smelly, sometimes noisy, but always embarrassing if you have to be with people.

> I used to get fart attacks – seizures of wind that might go on for hours – parp! parp! every few minutes. No wonder I became a bit of a hermit.

As recovery progresses, bowel actions settle down and return to normal – although for some people this can take a few years.

> Now I tend to get constipated around the time of ovulation and to get diarrhoea at the time of my period. I can tie it in with my menstrual cycle, and that is the pattern I had before I started taking the pills. So I'm back to normal, and I don't look on it as a problem any more.

BREATHING AND LUNGS

Breathing difficulties are very common in withdrawal. People feel that they have to gasp for air, as if the oxygen has somehow run out. They sigh continually in the effort to get more air in their lungs. It is as though the breathing mechanism has been disrupted.

> I'd have periods of thirty seconds when I'd stop breathing, to the point where I'd nearly black out. My breath would get really shallow and I could almost feel myself stop breathing and be unable to start again. It was as though the message from the brain to the lungs wasn't connecting and then would just stop. This was particularly shocking in bed at night, as I'd become aware of the fact that I'd stopped breathing and I'd have to restart myself by concentration on deep breathing.

I had episodes of great difficulty in breathing, or very shallow breathing, as though my lungs had been stitched up about an inch from the top and no longer had the capacity to hold very much air.

Lung infections, wheezing and asthma also affect quite a few people. These symptoms can develop later in the withdrawal.

It is certainly not advisable for a person with any lung weakness to take benzos. So many people I have spoken to who have taken benzos have got asthma or their existing asthma is much worse. I had very mild wheezing for a short time as a child but when I was on the pills I had pleurisy, and after I came off them I got it again, after which I was told I had developed asthma. I was given medication which made me feel ill, so I didn't take it. The asthma went away after almost a year, never to return.

BREASTS

A few women find that their breasts become heavy, painful and swollen, not just before a period but randomly, at any time. Sometimes one breast is more badly affected than the other. With this goes extreme breast sensitivity. Being touched, wearing a bra or tight clothing may be unbearable. Some women have lumpy breasts for which there is no explanation. These symptoms affect post-menopausal women as well.

My left breast was sore on and off for about two years. I used to dread my boyfriend hugging me because it hurt so much. I tried not to wince – I didn't like having to push him away. I had endless examinations and a mammogram – I was terrified I had cancer. Now my breasts are fine, quite normal.

I hated having my car seatbelt strapped over my boobs. I kept pulling it out and driving with it held away from my body with one hand. It must have looked silly and it was probably dangerous as well.

My breasts were supersensitive, so much so that I could not bear to lie in bed and feel the weight of my doona.

Note: all abnormal breast symptoms should be checked by a doctor. Never assume that they are just part of the withdrawal.

BRUISING

Spontaneous bruising – bruises that occur without cause, when you have not bumped yourself – plague some people in benzo withdrawal. These bruises usually seem to appear on the insides of the arms and legs, although they do occur on breasts, buttocks and elsewhere on the body. For others the problem is more that they seemed to bruise very easily: 'I could just walk past a chair and touch it a little bit heavier than usual and I'd get a purple-red bruise immediately.' This is no worse than a bit puzzling or inconvenient, but the spontaneous bruises can be alarming.

One summer morning when I was wearing shorts I glanced down at the inside of my thigh and saw a row of five dark bruise marks. It freaked me right out. I knew I hadn't knocked myself there. I'd read somewhere that spontaneous bruising was a symptom of leukaemia, and I said to myself, this is it. I dashed over to a local doctor's surgery – barged in while she was with another patient. She looked at my thigh, raised her eyebrows and said, 'Hmm, your boyfriend must have grabbed you too tightly.' I knew that wasn't true. Her lack of concern rubbed off on me – but even though I stopped worrying I was still mystified until I found out that spontaneous bruising is a symptom of tranquilliser withdrawal.

These bruises have a different appearance from an ordinary bruise.

> They were very dark in colour and they had a pinkish tinge to them. They didn't go the normal pattern of a bruise.

> These things aren't like bruises that happen when you bump yourself – they are painless and there is no lump or swelling. At first there's a faint mark or shadow on the skin which within a day darkens to a deep smudge. This lasts a few days, then it fades to a yellow patch which takes a little while longer to go away. They look horrible because they make such a contrast with that very white skin on the inner arms and legs.

As recovery proceeds, the bruises appear less and less often.

About the time they began to fade I came to value the bruises in a funny sort of way. They seemed like visible evidence that I wasn't imagining things – that something real was happening to my body. They also seemed to be a mark of progress. Slowly, slowly they became fewer and fewer until now I hardly ever get them. This cheered me up because it seemed like I was really getting somewhere.

CONCENTRATION AND METAL SHARPNESS

Poor concentration affects everybody in withdrawal, either while on benzos or when they are coming off. There is no mental sharpness – no ability to analyse, to see patterns and connections. Jobs done easily for years become a burden, and even simple household tasks seem insurmountable. If people push themselves – try hard to focus their thoughts – they can become sick or agitated.

'My mind wanders – I cannot concentrate'

Close mental application is impossible as people find they cannot stick to things. Some leave their jobs and look for an alternative they can manage. Reading habits gradually change – many stop reading altogether. They find it hard to write a letter let alone a report or essay. Often people can no longer do simple arithmetic – they can't even check their change or play games where they have to add numbers.

I didn't have any concentration for a very long time after I stopped taking benzos. Now, several years later, my concentration has improved a good deal, but I still have difficulty reading something very long because I can't stick to it, which makes me distracted and upset. I have to make a mental effort to concentrate on a complicated journal article. Pre-pills I might have had to make an effort to comprehend a complicated article, but it wasn't difficult to maintain concentration.

I couldn't think clearly for a long time. I was trying to do a university course by correspondence, and then I couldn't think logically. I would have to write down every single point in the margin so that I didn't repeat myself. I would read through the essay and I honestly did not know whether it made sense or not.

I had been a bookkeeper but I find doing the household accounts a nightmare. When I try to figure anything out I absolutely go to pieces; I shake and shiver and my head seems to bulge and thump, so I give up and come back to it again. I make mistakes, like one and one is three.

No mental sharpness

Perception and analytical abilities are lost; people find it almost impossible to do their jobs, deal with others and keep up an appearance of being alert and on the ball. It takes some time for people to recover these faculties, but many get back on track and into full or part-time employment. Others take longer.

I started to feel 'foggy' in the mornings when I got up. And then there were days when I would read through some work and I couldn't get a grip on it or I couldn't stick with a long and detailed conversation with a client – I thought I must be having a nervous breakdown but I didn't know why. I put it down to overwork, needing a holiday – that sort of thing.

My mental sharpness, clarity of thinking and perception became severely blunted causing me to leave my job which required all those skills. I started my own business after coming off Serepax, but my mind was numbed for years and I'm sure I was unemployable. I could somehow manage being my own boss because I wasn't under any pressure to perform – I could organise my hours better, but I can't imagine what my clients must have thought when I lost track of what they were saying. It is six years since I took my last Serepax and I still have some 'blurry' days.

It isn't only at work that people need a clear head. Simple everyday tasks like paying the gas bill or sorting through old photographs, jobs we take for granted, are daunting.

I'm a keen racing person and I can read the form guide very well these days whereas in the first year it may as well have been written in Chinese.

I really missed the dinner parties, with lots of stimulating conversation. My mind is not sharp enough now and I don't like going out any more – I'm embarrassed by my lack of social skills. I used to be really quick with repartee and now I can't sort through the ideas let alone make a witty rejoinder.

CONFIDENCE

Most people find that their self-confidence and self-esteem suffer badly during withdrawal. They lose confidence in their ability to do the ordinary everyday things which they have been doing competently for years: their work, social interactions – even the most basic tasks like housework or cooking.

Even the simplest things like cooking a chop . . . somehow I think that this lamb chop is not cooked as well as I could have done it – I have lost so many abilities. I couldn't teach now. I couldn't get up in front of people and perform in any way. When I think about all that – how I have lost all my confidence – that's when I feel despairing. I wonder whether it will ever come back again.

I became very apprehensive about being able to do the things I was supposed to, such as playing the organ at my local church – I kept wondering if I would be well enough. I dropped out of a few things; I always left an escape route so someone else could take over if I couldn't do it.

People become afraid to undertake anything in case they fail.

I wonder what is the point of even starting when I know I could collapse in a heap. I felt that I couldn't do anything, and so I didn't do anything in case I couldn't. My loss of confidence lasted quite a few years. I felt as though I'd fucked up and could never get back to where I was before I started taking the pills. At school I was king of the castle, but I felt I could never be a leader again.

A lot of energy goes into keeping up a facade of confidence, particularly for those who have challenging work commitments. In the long run, however, the struggle to overcome lack of confidence can be worthwhile in itself.

Confidence and self-esteem were probably the biggest casualty of all. Confidence went down to zero, and it takes a lot of work to get it back up again. Everyone I spoke to felt very worthless as an individual. You take thirty years or more to build yourself into the person your parents brought you up to be, and it takes five years for a pill to knock you back to zero. You then have to build yourself up again, dealing also with the guilt the pills have left you with. But it's a double-edged thing. The effort you put into coping with withdrawal will also help your self-esteem as well, so you do get a benefit out of it if you keep going. In any case there's no way back. When I was really low that was my question – what was my alternative? You either go forward or you don't go anywhere.

I didn't think I was good for anything, and I had to work very hard to hide that. The whole of life was hiding things, preventing people from finding out, putting on a normal face and doing normal things so that people wouldn't know what was wrong with you, so there's that hidden lack of self-confidence while trying to appear ordinary. The net result was that when I went for my second job I was enormously confident because I thought that if I got through that I can do anything. I did think that I had got through the worst of it, and I had.

CRYING JAGS

Coming off benzos seems to release emotions that have been suppressed for years, and many people find that tears are very close to the surface. They go through a period of extreme over-emotionality, having fits of crying excessively about things which normally would not touch them quite so deeply. Few see this as a problem though. It feels healthy and therapeutic, a step on the road to recovery.

Quite out of the blue I find tears leap to my eyes. It's like a great sadness welling up, but it's good to be able to feel again that way. I've been very moved sentimentally at times.

Sometimes I think I must be dehydrated because I cry so much. I cry at anything. I never watch the news because it upsets me too much, and I even cry at soaps. I had to give them up because they upset me too much.

I'm not a crying person but I did have some crying jags. I used to belong to Amnesty International, but at some stage during withdrawal I stopped writing letters and reading letters in the Amnesty journal because they were so specific about torture and I just couldn't take it. Now I have almost returned to normal apart from some small over-sensitivities.

For the ten years I was on the pills I don't think I ever cried, but when coming off and after I cried a lot, and occasionally I cry now, which is good. If I felt the need to cry before I took the pills I would repress it. While on the pills I didn't feel the emotion. Coming off I cried more than I needed. Now I cry when I need to.

DECISION-MAKING AND JUDGEMENT

Decision-making becomes difficult for most sufferers, either because they cannot think clearly or the mental effort is too much for them. It is one thing to agonise over the major issues, but not to be able to make a decision about which vegetables to cook for dinner or what shirt to put on in the morning makes people feel foolish and inadequate. Many lose confidence in their judgement and put off making up their minds or get someone else to help.

I remember years of being immobilised by the inability to make decisions, even simple decisions. I used to find myself poised in front of two different brands of breakfast cereals: which one would I take home? It was too big a decision to make. I felt like the donkey in Aesop's Fables which stood an equal distance between two bales of hay but couldn't make up his mind which one to eat and eventually starved to death through his lack of decision.

> I put everything off because I didn't trust my judgement. I could not get started on anything. Before I took pills, if I'd decided to buy a new car, I'd organise the paperwork and have the car by that night. Now, I can't make a decision about anything. I moved into this flat intending to stay for three months – I've been here two and a half years. I have some furniture which I haven't brought here – I can't make the decision about which day, what trailer and so on. Just simple decisions like that are too much for me.

Bad decisions

People find themselves making bad decisions. They go on spending sprees, buying things they later find they don't need or like. Some go on holidays in climates they have always disliked and a few buy houses in areas which are unsuitable. People occasionally leave their partners and later realise they may have made a mistake.

> I wasn't happy in my marriage but I think that taking the pills did not help me look at the problems we were having. In the end I left my husband, but I am now seeing him again and we are starting to talk and work things out.

> I made lots of really bad decisions while still on pills and later when I came off. I've bought

clothes that I wouldn't otherwise have bought in a
million years, and I've paid money for them that I
would find laughable. The damn things don't
even fit me and I don't even like them. I bought a
cardigan that I paid a lot of money for and I still
can't believe it. I loathe it. I wore it once and I
thought I looked like a circus clown. I've stopped
buying clothes. I'd rather other people made
decisions at present.

DEPRESSION AND SUICIDAL THOUGHTS

Benzodiazepines act as a depressant. After people
have fully recovered many look back and realise
that they endured low-grade depression that for
years took the pleasure out of life while they were
still on benzos.

It was not a deep depression, but rather a feeling
that everything had lost its point – nothing excites
you or thrills you or turns you on. It's like a giant wet
sponge has been put on everything. I'm still unin-
terested in things, and I used to be an energetic
person, a real goer.

After coming off the pills, depression about
being trapped in the withdrawal process itself is
not uncommon.

I get depressed when I reflect on my life situation
and this illness. It can manifest itself as physical
symptoms such as nausea which are added to the
rest of the withdrawal to produce a pretty nasty
cocktail. I feel like someone hanging on the edge of a

clifftop, slowly sliding down. This is very wearing-down.

I don't feel whole at all going through this with-drawal, and it makes me depressed. I have never had depression like this. I always got myself out of it before, but in withdrawal I could not do that.

But the deepest, darkest kind of depression in withdrawal is not 'about' anything external, any event in your life. It is spontaneous depression, caused by the biochemical disorder of with-drawal. It comes and goes at random. Those who suffer from this kind of depression – more aptly called despair – sometimes find it more unbear-able than physical pain.

Depression was very bad. A gloom would come over me, a blackness. I didn't want to talk. I'd go into myself. It is a feeling of total emptiness – a really ugly sort of feeling. It is worse than pain. I still get it but it is very gradually decreasing. The worst times are in the morning and between five and seven at night.

My first bout of severe depression started during my fourth month off pills – that's how clearly I remember it. It suddenly swept over me, a feeling of absolute despair and nothingness. It was a physical thing – I felt incredibly low and heavy. I could feel it choking me, blocking my throat. It was like a very bad pain – worse, actually. I was so crushed by that first depression, it never occurred to me to connect it with the benzos. I saw my doctor, who was very worried – referred me to a psychiatrist. I went once. Then after about a month or so it suddenly lifted, vanished as mysteriously as it came. I turned into a different person, started planning a birthday dinner. Not manic, just normally happy. Since then it has come back in random bouts. The awful thing is that when it comes I can never explain it away to myself as a symptom the way I can with most other things – it always feels as though my life has fallen into a black hole and I'll never escape.

Suicidal thoughts

Not surprisingly, people sometimes think about ending it all as they battle depression and chronic ill health during a protracted withdrawal period.

Yes, I have been suicidal. When you are ill for a very long time, you think it would be better to be dead. There is no pleasure in living, nothing to look forward to. You feel a burden on your family.

Others report 'spontaneous' suicidal impulses that are not related to feelings of sadness or despair about their lives, but caused by chemical changes in withdrawal.

For two years I was suicidal. Now when I get the weird thoughts I know it's not me, it's not the way I'm feeling today as a person, it's all a throw-back to rebound symptoms because you can often get thoughts without wanting them there. You can have a lovely sunny day, everything's going just great, and suddenly you feel like just killing yourself right in the middle of it.

Even those who are confident that they would never really kill themselves are aware that those dark impulses are something to be wary of.

I have never felt suicidal, never; but I can understand how people could feel that way. It is almost like an abstract thing – you feel that you have been taken over by a 'spirit'.

I knew I had to be on guard against those thoughts, that they were not to be trifled with. I used to divert my thinking with anything which would hold my attention – I found it hard to talk to people or read when I felt suicidal, so TV was the best for me.

But some people come very close to the brink – and a small minority actually attempt suicide.

One day I contemplated killing myself, and I thought, I can't. I was afraid of death and I thought that one day I might get better, and I thought of my children. They were the three things that held me together and stopped me doing it.

I know for a fact that the Mogadon altered my thinking. I did things on them that I never would have done off them. I told the doctor that I was worried about the way the pills were affecting my judgement and behaviour. I had suicidal thoughts by then. He said not to worry as no one ever died of

Mogadon. I had never had suicidal thoughts before when I had been depressed, so I was worried. By this time I wasn't able to make a normal decision and didn't seem to have any more emotion. All I could think of was that life was too painful and that I had had enough, so I rang up a taxi and went up to the hills and cut my wrists. However, my son followed me. When I realised what I had done, it was a terrible shock to me – what I had done to my children.

DEXTERITY AND MOTOR CO-ORDINATION
(household tasks, using machinery,
writing, spelling and numeracy)

Benzodiazepines affect the nervous system, so it is not surprising that dexterity and co-ordination deteriorate in withdrawal. Many people find they forget how to spell words they've known for years. Others can't add up their change and their writing is jerky and messy. They worry about becoming a danger to themselves and others. They have more accidents, at home, in the work-place and on the roads.

I had always been very quick – reflexes, responses, all that sort of thing. My job depended on it. I had to think on my feet. In the last six months on the pills I began lose all these skills as well as my co-ordination, to the point where there were days when I could no longer operate a simple telephone system. I would stare at it with all the lights flashing and not know how to transfer the calls. It was humiliating.

I transposed letters when writing and I still do that. I rarely did things like that before. My spelling and writing has deteriorated – it is worse when I'm having a bad day. I can see in my notes that my writing is poor. One of the kids picked up my shopping list one day and said, 'Mum, this isn't your usual neat writing.' I am often clumsy and walk into things.

My co-ordination is terrible – hopeless at doing jobs around the house. I'm having trouble stringing words together. I found it difficult to read and take in the information – as if my brain was somewhere else. My written skills were poor for some time; they are not as good as they were and I earned my living with them! Others in our support group are the same. There is a woman who can no longer sew. She can't work out the dressmaking pattern – where all the pieces fit. And she earned her living making clothes at one time.

DIZZINESS

Dizziness is a very common problem. People might feel slightly dizzy all the time, or have sudden attacks of severe dizziness. Suddenly standing up, standing in a queue or at a sporting function can make this symptom worse.

If I sat down I would feel better but if I had to keep standing I felt my head was starting to wobble, a bit like a small baby's does before they have the strength to hold it up. I looked in the mirror to check and my head was still; it was just the feeling of wobbling which made me feel dizzy.

Off-balance
Even sitting in a chair or lying in bed, people could feel off-balance. Feelings of uncertainty about where to put their feet makes walking hard.

> I often felt off-balance while standing and found it bizarre that at these times it was difficult for me to speak. Actually the closer to the ground I could get, the better I'd feel. A friend used to put me on a kitchen stool and I would feel terrible. I would get off it and sit down on the floor. I could have a much better conversation with her from there.

'The ground is moving'
People don't often actually fall, but they think they will because the ground does not feel either firm or solid.

> I used to feel like I was walking on cotton wool. I haven't got good balance any more – I feel like the ground is moving under me at times. I am a long way from recovery in this area, and I always wear flat shoes now.

DREAMS AND NIGHTMARES
Dreaming is often suppressed while people are taking benzos. When dreams return they can be enjoyable, vivid in colour and intensity. At other times dreaming is unpleasant and takes people back into the past, dredging up forgotten incidents.

192 The Accidental Addict

I hadn't dreamed for several years when I was on the pills. After I came off I had jumbled dreaming, and repetitive type dreams which went on for some years. After a while I started to dream about things which had happened years ago – when the kids were little.

I used to have dreams of hallucinatory brilliance but benzos have ruined another type of dream for me. Before I used Ativan, I would dream long detailed 'movies' which I found very creative.

I would sleep for about two hours, dream and wake up sweating. Then I would get up and sit in a chair for a few hours. I often had bad dreams. I would listen to the radio most of the night. I used to ring up some of those talk-back programs.

Nightmares

Some people are afraid to go to sleep because of their nightmares. Women have dreams about their children being hurt or killed. Men often dream about being killed or trapped. For a few people these nightmares continue after they are awake.

I started to have these nightmares; even when I woke screaming they didn't stop. Sometimes the nightmare continued for ten minutes after I woke up. It was always about walking off scaffolding, or stepping out of a plane, and so bloody real that my wife would have to repeatedly slap my face to help me get rid of it. Cold-packs, wet cloths, ice blocks, anything, to take my mind off it.

During the first years of the withdrawal, my past in London during the Blitz came back very vividly with claustrophobic dreams of being buried under piles of rubble.

I slept well but I had a lot of nightmares. Really bizarre dreams like I saw Jesus Christ standing at the doorway of the bedroom surrounded by a big bright light. I'd have nightmares about the kids being killed or dying in their sleep or having horrific diseases.

I had terrible nightmares and I would sleep-walk too. One night my son and his girlfriend heard me screaming, and found me crouching down on the floor saying that someone was trying to get in the window. And I often got out of bed and would be found standing somewhere in the house.

EYES AND VISION

Blurred, foggy or fading vision

Episodes of blurred vision and difficulty in focusing bother most sufferers. People might visit an oculist several times to have their eyes tested.

I had three pairs of glasses made during early withdrawal, but not one of them was quite right – then I realised it was the benzos playing havoc with my eyes.

I had double vision as well as blurred vision, and at one stage I was given bifocal glasses. Now my vision has improved so much that I no longer need the glasses.

I finally asked my oculist whether the withdrawal could be affecting my eyes. He said it could. He told me that plenty of his patients had trouble while they were on those rotten pills, and that I shouldn't bother to change my glasses again until I was fully recovered.

While blurred vision seems to affect the function of the eye itself, foggy vision is 'out there' in the environment, and might include an impression that the room is full of smoke or mist – you find yourself always trying to clean your glasses because they seem smoky or smeared, or there's a cloud in front of your eyes. A dimming of vision is also experienced.

I had this funny dimming out of vision. It was like the weather is changing and cloud is replacing the sunlight. It's like a whole change of focus.

My left eye would seem to just grey out and fade. I was sure I was dying or going blind. It really scared me – I'd keep blinking frantically, trying to correct it. But when I closed my right eye, I found that I could see perfectly well from that dim left eye. I used to have fits of intense anxiety when I was quite sure my symptoms were due to a brain tumour. These terrors disrupted my life and made me very miserable. After about two years off the pills my vision returned to normal.

Acute sensitivity to light
People in withdrawal tend to dread the bright, sunny days that everyone else welcomes as 'lovely weather'. Strong light may induce extreme disorientation, anxiety, sweating, even nausea.

> For a year after coming off my pills I wore dark glasses even in the house – sometimes I even watched TV with them on!

> I needed photochromic lenses all the time. I could not stand being in the sun at all, whereas earlier in my life I enjoyed it. Driving in glaring light was particularly hard. Only after three years off the pills was I able to drive without sunglasses, even in winter.

Some artificial light sources also cause discomfort, particularly fluorescent light which makes many people feel twitchy and uneasy. Computer screens can be difficult to cope with, as are oncoming headlights when driving at night. The repeated flashing of the lights as they rush past cause panicky feelings and a fear of losing control of the car.

Red, sore, watery eyes
Many people are plagued by red, pimply, weepy eyes.

> My eyes were constantly red. I often got little sties or infected pimples around the rim of the eye and sometimes inside it. It was most unattractive, and it embarrassed me. This lasted for about two years – after that it was fine.

Eyes can be painful as well as red and unsightly, feeling sore, gritty, itchy, grating and burning – rather like bad conjunctivitis. These benzo-affected eyes produce a lot of liquid, usually referred to as 'gunge', 'gunk' or 'bogglies'.

> There was a stage at about one year off the tablets when my eyes felt like they were full of ground glass.

> My eyes felt poisonously sore, with a bitter smarting quality – as though someone had thrown battery acid in them.

> My eyes were so watery that even at four years off pills my daughter would ask, 'Are you crying, Dad?'

Perceptual distortions and visual hallucinations
Many people find that their visual perceptions are no longer reliable. Things seem to be moving as they look at them. Their spatial sense suffers, making them clumsy and awkward: 'I kept bumping into walls like a drunk.' Driving skills can be badly impaired by these perceptual distortions, making it hard to negotiate tunnels and traffic lanes.

> When I looked at objects they would seem to be shifting. A table might seem to be a foot off the ground, or a white line on the road apparently moving up and down.

> I can be clumsy with coffee cups and lemonade, not putting them down on the table properly. Things are not in their proper perspective; you

> click yourself and you think, that's not right. I had
> never had any such problems before I started
> taking those pills.

> I could hardly drive at all because I couldn't tell if the
> traffic lanes were 20 or 200 yards ahead of me.
> After many years of safe driving I had two road
> accidents during withdrawal.

Perceptual distortions can also make it difficult to
talk to others in social situations. People around
you start to look distorted, or to seem smaller or further away.

Hallucinations are rare, but they do happen –
and they can be terrifying.

> I saw a 'split' in my eye with a jagged streak like a
> lightning bolt through my pupil. I also had a flick-
> ering before my eyes like the stardust from Fanta-
> sia.

> I had a lot of visual disturbances while on and
> while withdrawing from the pills. It still happens, and
> it'll come on out of the blue. First I see shimmering
> lights, then I develop tunnel vision, then my right eye
> dims. The only thing to help is to go to bed and
> sleep for half an hour.

FACE AND APPEARANCE

During withdrawal faces are often puffed out or
bloated and distorted. Skin colour varies from 'a
dreadful yellow coffee colour' through shades of
beetroot red and putty grey to ashen pale.

The colour of my skin has changed. I look sallow, just like a bowl of porridge. The colour comes and goes. My face is very puffy. I look in the mirror and say, who's that fat lady? Age certainly hasn't enhanced you. When I'm feeling well I look better and the puffiness has quite gone.

During my first year off the pills I noticed that my face was all puffed up and squashy looking. It seemed to be pulled across to the left. I could hardly recognise myself in the mirror. I felt embarrassed – being so sick was bad enough without looking like a monster as well. It was strange because it would vary from day to day. Sometimes I'd wake up and there to my great relief would be my own face and pink skin again.

FATIGUE AND LETHARGY

Fatigue and lethargy are two of the most common and persistent symptoms that strike people in withdrawal. Fatigue is a weariness from bodily or mental exertion, whereas lethargy is a state of drowsy dullness and apathy. These symptoms very often appear in the early days of taking benzos and can disappear overnight only to return several weeks later. Many people are so weakened by these two debilitating symptoms that they have to stop work or are unable to look after their families.

Fatigue

Benzo fatigue is not a normal, pleasant sort of tiredness – it can be a general weariness or total exhaustion, and sometimes a stressed-out feeling as well. Sleeping is the only way some people cope with this symptom. Others feel weary but can't sleep because they feel jittery or agitated. People report a mental exhaustion; they are able to do physical work but their minds seem to shut down: 'The tiredness is in my head, it isn't my body that's tired.' Fatigue can strike at any time – it is not necessarily the result of effort, although exertion can bring it on.

I have to regulate my life so that I don't exert myself too much. For example, while on holidays with my older sister I noticed that she could do things like have a shower before tea. It would exhaust me to do that. I try to make myself take a walk every day, but I haven't got a lot of energy. In the mornings after I've washed the dishes and hung out the clothes I'm exhausted. My mother, when she was in her seventies, could run rings round me.

I find having a shower and washing my hair really exhausting. I wait until the afternoon when I feel a little stronger. If I do it in the morning, say at nine, I have to lie down until lunchtime.

I was so tired I was having to go to sleep at 7.30 at night which was causing problems with my husband because I'd be asleep and he'd want to, you know . . . For the first two years I just slept and slept. Walking and just going for a drive in the car would tire me out.

I was always weak and fatigued. It went on for several years before I felt a spring in my step. It's a feeling that all your tissues are dying; that you can't send electricity to any of your muscles to make them function; that you're always dragging yourself around – dragging yourself out of bed – dragging yourself along the street.

Sometimes I feel as I did the first few weeks after major surgery. Not just tired but completely depleted of all my blood, as if some vampire had sucked me dry. It's debilitating. It doesn't necessarily last the whole day, and I don't have it day in and day out, it just comes and goes. I can be out visiting and it will suddenly come, and I want to lean back and close my eyes and crawl back inside myself and go to sleep.

Lethargy
People feel so sleepy that they regularly doze during the day. Apathy and a total disinterest in what is going on means that they just can't be bothered. It is too much effort. They can often sit, staring into space.

I can be totally lethargic – just sit here and do nothing, not move a muscle. The place can be filthy. Other days I will have it spotless and it will smell so fresh. I love watching football but when I feel like this I just don't want to go out. I was never like this before.

I used to have such extreme lethargy that to wash a pair of socks or knickers was too much for me. I remember at that time we moved house and it was such an ordeal. My husband used to

help me with the housekeeping. I just could not
do it.

Exercise and exertion

As the majority of people suffer from a general
tiredness or exhaustion, they find most forms of
exercise impossible in the first few months of
withdrawal. Digging in the garden, vacuuming the
house, chopping firewood seem to be almost
impossible for some time. That kind of exertion
can make people very ill indeed.

> I couldn't exercise at all for over a year. For the
> next few years I used to try to go for a walk, and after
> about fifteen minutes I could feel withdrawal
> symptoms coming on. I would start to get dizzy,
> then my head would start to ache. My legs would
> feel like lead and I'd start to feel depersonalised.
> For some reason, I kept on trying, month after
> month and year after year. Now, at six years off
> pills I can walk, fast, for about forty minutes, but that
> is it. After that, I'm starting to get woozy.

> I couldn't do anything which involved lifting my
> arms or climbing stairs. Any exertion exhausted
> me for a couple of years. I was helping a friend to
> move and they asked me to carry some heavy car-
> tons – it knocked me out for a week.

Too much too soon

If you have been unable to exercise and have been
feeling ill for some time, it is easy to be misled
when you feel a little better. It is common for
people to take that opportunity, go shopping or

out to dinner, only to find that halfway through
the meal, they feel exhausted and have to go
home.

> At about ten months off pills I had the first flush of
> energy and I was kicking a football. It nearly killed
> me. I could hardly walk around for the next few
> days.

> I had no energy for a couple of years and then I
> started to feel a lot better. But as soon as I did feel
> good, I always seemed to forget that I was recovering
> from benzos, and I would carry on my life as
> others do – working all day and then some house-
> work and occasionally going out. I found I could
> not do that – it brought on many of the symptoms
> which I thought had gone for good. I still had to
> live quietly – not going out if I had to work; that
> sort of thing. You can't always do that and then
> you have to pay the price. It has been a long haul
> and I still have to be careful.

FLU-LIKE SYMPTOMS

People often think they are coming down with a
bout of flu because they feel hot and cold all over,
burning and sweaty. But nine times out of ten it
lasts a day or so, then peters out. These instances
are very common.

> You would feel like you had a real bad dose of the
> flu: achey, sniffly, sore throat. But full-blown flu
> doesn't eventuate – it's just withdrawal symp-
> toms, and then they go away till next time.

GENITALS

Chronic infections, soreness, rashes and itchiness affect both men and women. Some men have aching testes and penile numbness.

> I had a lot of thrush infections while I was on the pills. I had an itchiness and burning which drove me crazy.

> There was an initial constant all-over pain that finally settled as pelvic pain. I never knew exactly where it was – it was hard to work out if it was in the vagina or some place else. Other people have this too.

> Numb dick for about a year. The sensation was quite odd. I remember how different it felt when it went away.

HAIR

Hair can become dull and lifeless. Even worse, it thins or falls out by the handful, although this is uncommon.

> My hair lost all its natural bounce. The hair-dresser asked me if I was taking anything as she said my hair was really 'relaxed' – it had no life. I had a really strong perm and it didn't take properly.

> My hair was worse after I stopped taking benzos. It has thinned out quite a bit over the past few years. I had a thick head of hair before. My dad has still got all his hair and I have asked Mum about her parents and baldness doesn't seem to

run in the family. I'm hoping it will grow back because I have noticed that the thinning has stopped now.

My hair really worried me – I developed a bald patch and when it grew back it was grey.

HEAD

Almost all sufferers describe some sort of head symptom: pain, pressure, strange sensations as well as 'electrical activity'. These symptoms are particularly terrifying because they strike at the core of a person's control.

Headache and pain

This pain is not like an ordinary headache. It is often much more severe and lasts longer. Some people report having continuous headaches for weeks, even months. There are blocks of pain which throb, making heads feel heavy, and constant dull aches as well as tight bands of pain. Sometimes there can be a burning sensation deep inside the head. Many people fear that they have developed a serious illness.

I thought I was having a stroke. I had constant headaches for three and a half years. Sometimes I couldn't stand it because it was so painful. I had a break from the headaches for a few months, then they came back but they were not so severe.

My headache lasted for a long time and in desperation I went to a neurologist who reassured me that there was nothing lethal in my head. The pain started a few days after I stopped taking Valium and lasted for two years. It was always there when I woke up in the morning and sometimes it lurked all day, never becoming more severe. Other times it became worse during the day until it was unbearable. It could start as a dull overall ache and then, a few hours later, move to one localised spot, like over an eye or in my temples. It became more severe if I was tired or stressed. I also had short, sharp flashes of pain. For the next four years I had headaches intermittently, but what really upset me was if I concentrated for an hour or so, the same type of headache would return.

I felt like my head was being squashed or pulverised. It was as though someone was inside my head with a vice which they kept tightening.

Pressure

It was like my head would swell up and burst, then go down again – as if someone had a balloon inside my head and was pumping it up, then letting it down.

There was so much pressure in my head I felt I needed a pressure valve to relieve it. I had it for a couple of years. It became a part of my life and made me feel fuzzy all the time. Now I get it back if I have to concentrate too hard on anything complicated. The pressure and fuzziness come back as if my brain cannot cope.

Weird sensations

Sufferers have bizarre feelings inside their heads, as though something has shifted from one side to the other. Their scalps can seem stretched or have prickling sensations, and sometimes they feel there is hot water dribbling through their hair.

> I found it hard to explain the weird feeling to my family. It was a feeling of being off-balance, like when your sinuses or ears are blocked and you blow through your nose to clear them. I've recently had an awful feeling of being off-centre, as though my head was cut in half and then cut in quarters, and that all the quarters were quite symmetrical, but that someone had moved them slightly out of alignment so that they were not quite parallel.

> I had a terrifying sensation of my head and visual field being flattened down in front of me, as though the whole front of my forehead was just being crushed down in a diagonal way and I could only see out from underneath it – like a Picasso face.

'Floaty' feelings

Within their own homes people feel reasonably secure, but outside, sometimes even in their own gardens, a 'floaty' head makes the world a very uncertain place.

> My head often feels fuzzy, like there is a cloud on top of it. Today it feels disconnected from my body, as though it is in space. I always feel out of control when these wafty feelings take over.

A lot of the time my head feels as if it is floating – just drifting a little way from my body. It makes working hard when I have to walk across the showroom floor to serve the customers. The simplest of acts, such as walking down the street, is stressful as I worry whether I might faint or stumble and maybe fall and make a fool of myself.

'Fireworks in the head'

Bursts of electrical activity in the head seem to come out the blue. What you are doing does not seem to cause them – you can be reading, watching TV or peeling the potatoes – but tiredness and stress seem to aggravate them. Some people see flashes of light, others can actually feel a disturbance.

It starts on the right side of my head and runs a crazy pattern right across my skull, like you might draw a flash of lightning. My eyes flicker and things actually appear to move on the table before me.

A thing would suddenly go off in my head like electric fireworks, or sometimes if felt like a jolt from an electric cattle prod. Then for the next few days I'd have aftershocks, especially if I turned my head too abruptly to one side. This made me feel precarious – I'd be too scared to move in case I set off another shock.

I hated the electric shocks – it was like Guy Fawkes night when we were kids, but in my head. I thought I was becoming an epileptic and I was sure I would have a fit. That never happened and slowly the fireworks died down.

HEARING
Tinnitus (ringing in the ears)
Ringing, humming, buzzing, whining or simply 'noises in the ears' provide unwanted background noise for many people in withdrawal. Sometimes tinnitus is worse at night, just as heads hit the pillow. It can be brought on by stress or exhaustion, or it may come and go completely at random: 'suddenly something will go ping, and there it is'.

> I had tinnitus of a fairly simple sort – one high-pitched noise, not a cacophony. It was unpleasant but not unbearable – I could always work or talk or carry on. It was disturbing because I didn't know what it was – I'd never had it in my life before. I couldn't explain it just by saying I'm anxious or tired. It was persistent for 12 to 15 months; now it's intermittent.

Over-sensitivity to sound
Hearing can become super-acute to the point where it is 'as though you can hear things with your whole body'. Normal sound levels from TV and radio seem to be turned right up, while loud noise may cause real physical pain. Noisy public places such as restaurants and theatre foyers are also hard to bear. This is not only because of the general noise, but because it can be very distressing to have to cope with more than one person talking at once.

Before, I used to play happily with my grandchildren, but now I just wish they'd stop talking. When it's very noisy I just want to hang on to myself and crawl into a ball. I want to be part of it because I want to be part of life, but I can't join in making the noise. I want to protect myself.

Aversion to music

It is common for people who once loved music to find that they cannot stand listening to it.

I was always very keen on music, but during the first two years of my recovery I couldn't tolerate it at all; it seemed to madden me.

Music was always a part of this house, but now it makes me too nervous and it makes me too sad.

It may be that during withdrawal music over-stimulates the already fragile nervous system; it is simply too emotionally penetrating.

At about a year off pills I went to a musical play about the life of Edith Piaf. An actress was singing Piaf's songs. I felt as though the circuits of my mind and body were electrically wired up to the music. It was unbearably painful and disturbing. I started to panic and I had to get out.

As time passes, delight in music gradually returns.

In music I now hear things I haven't heard before, or not with the same depth or emotional impact. I've been looking for the perfect hi-fi for years, and now it's right here in my head. It's like a new adventure for me to hear what music's really like.

HEART AND PULSE

Palpitations, racing hearts, missed beats, and heart arrhythmia can start soon after taking the first benzo. Later, when people try to come off the pills, they can have attacks of palpitations that are so severe that they are hospitalised. Sleep may be disturbed when the natural heart rhythm is punctuated by missed beats and a racing pulse.

Palpitations and racing hearts

These are especially unnerving, because they might mean imminent death. Most people can't think, can't function – all they can do is panic.

> I had palpitations for years and thought, I am only thirty, how can I be having a heart attack? I was terrified, waiting for my heart to explode. How could it keep beating?

> Just as I was falling asleep I would wake up with a start, palpitations would be freaking me right out. I would have to talk to myself – tell myself that I was in my own bed and it would be okay. It was a terrifying feeling and made me afraid to go to sleep.

> I am still troubled by my heart racing. It seemed to be racing all the time at work. I think over the years of how many times it has been like that and I

think, hell, I'm frightened that I *will* have a heart attack. I was sent for an ECG but the doctor couldn't find a problem. My heart is racing where it should be idling, like I've just done the hundred-metre dash. It is not as bad in the morning but seems to build during the day.

Heart arrhythmia, thumps and irregular beats

I was rushed to hospital and I don't know how my heart didn't give out as it was thumping so much. I had heart thumps and irregular beats which lasted for months.

I had a sensation of feeling my blood going around my body. It would hit a spot and 'bump'; I could actually time it around my body. I had it for about six years and particularly after exercise. It is so good to be well again – I play golf now without any problem.

Blood pressure

A minority of people develop high blood-pressure while on benzos and when they come off.

I was often concerned by my high blood-pressure. It would sky-rocket – I didn't have a problem before I was on benzos.

JAW

Severe jaw pain and neuralgia are very common. There is numbness, as well as stiffness and prickling sensations, and the joints often ache.

I had a stiff jaw and face. A bit like when we used to cover our faces with plaster of paris, as kids.

I had severe pain in my right mandibular joint for years after I came off the pills. It was particularly bad in the morning when I woke up. At times I would get this excruciating pain in my jaw – not like toothache, more like I had been punched in the jaw.

LEFT/RIGHT-SIDED SYMPTOMS

One side of the body feels different to the other, or symptoms may affect one side only: 'I'd get terrible pains in my right breast but the left one would be perfectly fine.' These symptoms occur only rarely but when they do, people are frightened and disorientated.

Sometimes it was a feeling of pressure in my head, arm and leg. Other times it was like an anaesthetic wearing off all the way down the left side. It could be a weakness, aching or pain. I used to get very upset when I had it until I read an article about a woman describing her withdrawal symptoms, one of which was pins and needles all down one side of her body. That story gave me hope. In the beginning it happened any time but now it's more when I'm stressed, but not always. It can last three or four hours and comes and goes very suddenly.

I was frightened by my symptoms. My migraines were always on the right side. My face would go numb on that side and the tunnel vision would be more one-sided. When this first happened I thought I was having a stroke.

Left/right-sided confusion can lead to unexpected difficulties.

I must have my cup on my right side – I can't pick it up with my left; and I'm left-handed as a rule. It's as though the left- and right-hand spheres have their wires crossed.

When I was going to the cinema or visiting, it was often tricky to sit just in the right spot. I solved the problem by arriving at a restaurant first so that I could secure a seat where I felt most comfortable as I found it hard to communicate with people on my right.

MANIC EPISODES AND MOOD SWINGS

Episodes of manic exhilaration very often occur as the complete opposite of benzo lethargy and depression. Many people worry about talking too fast, looking spun-out and feeling elated when there is no reason at all for euphoria. But there are some who so enjoy these manic states that they have very little awareness that playing loud music or vacuuming their house at three in the morning drives their family or flatmates mad.

During the day I could hardly drive to the local milkbar. But very late at night I would find myself driving around the streets at high speeds bopping along to loud heavy metal music on the radio. One night, I even drove over the West Gate Bridge!

I had no job, no prospects because I was too ill to work and here I was on top of the world, talking nineteen to the dozen about buying a new house – crazy stuff!

The mania which seizes people for no reason disappears the same way, to be replaced by lethargy, doubt and misery. These extremes of emotion can often make people ill.

I had periods of manic elation for the first six months. It would buzz me right out – I could not contain it; like everything good had happened to me at once. But it would leave me feeling exhausted and depressed.

I am very careful not to stay out late at parties, or wind myself up in any way; if I do, the go-fast feeling returns. Relaxation methods are no good to me when I'm in that 'high' state. I've tried everything to bring myself down, but only time can do it. When I'm manic I don't sleep, then afterwards I'm a zombie.

Mood swings

I did not have mood swings before I took pills – now I get very bitter. I can change my mood so quickly, from being pleasant to saying nasty things. Then I think, I didn't mean that, and I cry and cry. I never was like that before, and I do say that the tablets made that difference to me because I don't think a person changes that much.

My mood swings were disastrous for my social life. I can go out with a person happy as anything at the beginning of the night. Then I change to just having to get away. I've been out with a girl and just had to get up and leave the money on the table in a restaurant and go. It took some years for my moods to return to normal but now I'm okay most of the time.

MEMORY

While long-term memory is almost unaffected, short-term memory is so badly affected people forget what they've said and forget what they've read. Time and time again, they buy the same items at the supermarket, catch the wrong trams and trains and get off at the wrong stops. One woman bought five vacuum cleaners. Not only does this harm relationships because people naturally get offended, it also interferes with competence at work. A fear of developing Alzheimer's disease is common.

I feel I have caused offence and lost friends because of my poor memory. I forgot arrangements, I forgot names, I forgot questions. I am two years off my pills and I still have problems with short-term memory. People tell me things but I can't remember having asked the question – they think I'm not interested in the information they're giving me.

I am in the ambulance service. My memory is totally unreliable and that upsets me. At times it can be so bad that I can't remember what I did yesterday, but half an hour later, I may be able to remember it quite clearly. On bad days it really worries me at work: for instance, if we transport eight patients during the day, I can't remember one of them – not one.

During the last years on benzos I know that although I was working very hard and doing a lot of overtime, I was working at half-cock all the time – I wasn't really on top of it. I was coping on the surface but inside it was panic. I wasn't acknowledging it at the time. By working overtime I managed to keep up. I was losing my grip because people would come to me for advice or information and I couldn't remember what had been arranged or said. I would have to keep notes of everything and look things up all the time. I lost files and couldn't keep it all together.

How they cope
People manage their deteriorating short-term memories in different ways.

I started making notes about everything. I had notes in my car to remind me of my calls. Then, after I'd called on a client, I had to make notes about everything that was said. I left little clues out: for example, if I had to take something somewhere I would leave it in front of the door at home – I would have to step over it to get out. If I left it on the bench in the kitchen I would forget it. It became a family joke.

I have been off Valium for some years and still have trouble with my short-term memory. I have to cover up a lot when I'm teaching. I have little strategies for concealing the fact that my short-term memory is not very good. I can't retain some information for more than half an hour and sometimes I cannot remember what day it is.

MENSTRUATION

Menstrual problems can occur for so many different reasons in women of different ages that it is risky to attribute any problems purely to benzos. However, some women do start to suffer from problem periods while they are on the pills which go back to normal after withdrawal.

My menstrual cycle was very disturbed for a very long time. I started having a period every three weeks and everything seemed to speed up. This had never happened before. I also had very heavy bleeding and constant thrush which would not go away for more than a day or two no matter what I did.

I had menstrual problems on the pills – I'd go for a month and not have a period then have one the next month, so it was always very irregular. Before I was on the pills it might go a week either way, but on the pills it might be two or three weeks out of kilter, and the cramps were worse. It was also very much heavier and it would last longer. Coming off the pills it seemed to get back into a more regular pattern. This took about six months or so, though after that I'd have bouts where it would get out of synch again.

My flow has been very light but at the beginning of this year it started to get very heavy. I've had some small variation, like three days early or two days late. I have had it twice in the one month. It is really heavy the first two days, then light for three days. You feel very weak those first couple of days. It is only a short period now.

MOTIVATION AND ENTHUSIASM

Everyone suffers from some loss of motivation and enthusiasm in withdrawal. Careers and home life can be badly affected when keenness ebbs away.

My loss of motivation was so bad that it affected my drive for promotion at work. I have been doing my job for fourteen years, and it is second nature to me, but I don't have any ambition to go any further; there's no motivation or enthusiasm for it.

A variation of the motivation problem is having the desire to do things but lacking the will. One woman said it was like being immobilised or becalmed – you simply cannot make yourself do anything.

There were so many things I wanted to do but somehow I just couldn't. I became a top-class pro-crastinator. It's getting better but it's still there. I would think about knitting something or starting a class; just something personal for me. I'd get bouts of enthusiasm and go out and buy heaps of material to make the girls some clothes, but I wouldn't have the energy to do the sewing. Then I'd feel guilty for spending all that money.

I can't get down to doing things, I can't get started. Motivation comes and goes. There's been an underlying lethargy and letting things rest because I'm too ill to do anything else. Also I don't push the boat out because I know the storm is going to be there, so I stay in the harbour.

But like other powers lost during withdrawal, motivation returns.

I'm a lot more motivated now as I get better and stronger. I had the motivation to go through with the withdrawal all along, but it was very hard to show enthusiasm . . . you just can't express it, you're too tired and it takes so much air to talk.

I was feeling so crook that I had no motivation, but as my health improves so does my energy and desire to do things. I want to go for it a lot of the time now.

MOUTH AND TONGUE

Pins and needles or numbness around the mouth and lips create problems for some people coming off benzos. Mouths may feel frozen, so that talking becomes awkward and eating messy – even painful.

I thought I was smiling, but wasn't. I had my photo taken with friends imagining I was giving this nice big smile but when I looked at the photograph there was no smile at all – the mouth and face were as if paralysed.

I had episodes of not being able to move my mouth. It felt as if it had forgotten its job. I would be speaking, then out of the blue, my mouth seemed to stop working – it would feel odd, sort of heavy, and my lips felt thick. I used to hit my mouth as if I could jolt it into working again.

I misfired all the time, for years. I grabbed my cheek instead of the food and was continually burning my mouth and throat with hot tea because my lips were numb.

Many people have too much saliva and are continually wiping the corners of their mouths – whereas others suffer from dry mouths. A few unfortunates have both. Mouth and tongue ulcers are also a common irritant.

I had too much saliva, as if I'd had just walked past the most delicious-smelling pastry shop and my mouth was watering. A person in one of the support groups named this 'washing-machine mouth'.

Tongue

My tongue feels alien, really different – it's not the tongue I remember. I notice it all the time and it gets in the way. I have no control over it and have trouble pointing it or curling it.

I felt my tongue was too big for my mouth, making it difficult to speak and swallow. It was even worse when it was numb and tingly. There was a layer of nasty yellow fuzz on the back of it for months.

MUSCLES AND JOINTS

Severe muscle and joint pain, spasm, tension and weakness are all very common. Muscle pain is often a general dull ache but at other times it can be particularly severe, especially in the neck and shoulders. Wrists, elbows, knees and ankles can also be very painful for the first years off pills.

You should have seen me getting out of the car – I was like an old man. My thighs, shoulders, and back were particularly bad. Another muscle problem was a feeling that someone had painted diagonal sashes across my chest and started hammering on them – a pain across all the muscles of my chest.

One of the worst things about coming off the pills was the terrible tightness at the back of the neck, between the skull and the neck. I felt as though it was screwed right up. I had that for months.

I had bad joint pains, like having the flu. It was bad in the hips and knees – an awful aching in the joints which went on for a long time. I still get it now if I get tired but not as much. It has gradually got better.

Muscle spasm and tension

People often wake up in the morning with cramps in their legs or tight knots in their necks and shoulders.

> Even during the night I had muscle spasm. I would have to stretch myself and crack my back to try and get relief. I never had trouble like this before I took benzos.

> My muscles were so tight I could not control the pen. My writing would go wonky and I couldn't keep to a straight line. I had to continue to write because I was at work and often someone was watching me. My arm and hand felt so taut – almost like the muscles had gone solid. I use a word processor now, but for the first few years it was impossible.

Muscle weakness

Weak muscles can make the simplest tasks difficult in the early stages of withdrawal. Just to get up out of a chair or hold your head up is too much at times. Any activity which involves raising the arms above the head is completely exhausting.

> I used to walk my son to school, not a difficult walk, and by the time I'd get home I'd just flop into a chair. It was tiring to peg clothes on the line. Even now my husband will peg the washing out.

> My neck muscles are very weak; if I get tired I have to rest my head on the back of the chair – or slide right down in the chair.

NUMBNESS/PINS AND NEEDLES

Numbness and pins and needles in all parts of the body and on the skin are very common in benzo withdrawal. Only one hand, one foot, half the nose or one leg may be affected. This is quite distinct from symptoms of 'normal' anxiety and over-breathing which cause numbness and pins and needles in both hands or both feet at once.

> I felt unnerved by the lack of feeling in my right foot. It happened occasionally while I was on the pills but much more often after I came off them. I felt like I was dragging it – it seemed bigger than my other foot too. I thought I might have a neurological disease, so I went to the doctor for tests and was relieved to find out I was all right. He couldn't explain the sensation of numbness though. I stuck a pin in my foot once and I could feel it but the sensation was quite different to pricking my other foot.

A loss of sensation in any part of the body can make movements like driving a car feel awkward. People mumble through numb lips and are prone to little mishaps because they cannot feel their fingers.

> I tried to treat my numbness as a bit of a joke. My fingers, nose and cheekbones were often numb. I used to put my fingers up to my face and think, oh, that's a lovely little nose, and I'd have to go to the mirror to reassure myself that I still had my big hooter.

There is something very disconcerting about not quite being able to feel the accelerator when I'm driving my car. It's a not-completely-in-control feeling. I constantly wiggle my toes, trying to get some sort of sensation back to sense how hard to push the pedals.

I had bouts of pins and needles all over my body and I was frightened when they were in my head. I had them for years and then one day they were gone.

PANIC ATTACKS

Everyone experiences nervousness and panicky feelings at some time. This is a normal response to stressful situations such as exams or job interviews. An anxiety or panic attack feels similar, but is much more intense. Its onset is sudden and often without cause, and it usually lasts for a few minutes. The symptoms are: shaking, palpitations, difficulty breathing, chest pain or discomfort, a choking feeling, dizziness, unreality, pins and needles, faintness and sweating. People can be terrified they are going to die or go crazy during an attack. It destroys self-confidence and control, making some people want to run to safety. Others are so struck by fear, they can't move at all. This is a very common benzo withdrawal symptom.

I would start sweating and gasping, and a choking feeling comes on. I start shaking and I feel like I might faint. I'm frightened of what someone might do to me, and I am scared to talk to anyone – I don't want anyone to come near me.

Panic attacks can occur within weeks of people starting benzos, making them afraid they are having a heart attack or nervous breakdown: 'After about two weeks on benzos, I had a panic attack and thought I was dying.' However, panic attacks most often occur as soon as people start to withdraw from the pills.

> I had been on benzos for about a year when I got the first attack. I now realise I was withdrawing during the day because I was taking the tablet at night. After I came off benzos, I had the attacks mainly at night – they used to wake me up, sometimes twice in the one night. They didn't seem to be associated with a nightmare, more like a short chemical disturbance in the brain.

Some people think their panic attacks are caused by feeling out of control. Such symptoms as 'floaty' head and feeling unsteady on their feet, blurred vision and faintness, make them uncertain and anxious, bringing on panic. Others think their attacks are caused by feelings of agoraphobia or claustrophobia.

It is possible to learn techniques such as deep breathing and positive self-talk which help to cope with panic attacks.

PARANOIA

The fear that other people are talking about or laughing at you can often be heightened during withdrawal. There is also a tendency to worry excessively over things said or done because you are sure you have offended someone or made a fool of yourself. A small number of people experience violent paranoid fears and imaginings.

> I feel that people are watching me. Even when I've got nice clothes on I think my fly is undone or I've dropped sauce down my front. I was never like that before. I try to force myself to get over that fear by wearing things like jeans that really do have a big rip in them. I go down the street and people are looking at me but at least there's something to look at. I come back and I've got the sweats and the shakes.

> I thought everything was my fault. I tended to agonise over everything. You are terribly guilty about everything. If I hadn't done this or that, this wouldn't have happened. You are constantly evaluating everything you say and do. I tell myself to stop but I can't.

> I had dreadful paranoia and bizarre thoughts. At one time while travelling on a bus I became convinced that a teenage boy opposite me had a gun and was going to kill everyone on the bus. I sat there and prepared to die. Suddenly the paranoid thought disappeared as quickly as it had appeared.

PHOBIAS

Phobias other than agoraphobia and claustrophobia are common. People dislike making or even answering telephone calls. Bathrooms, baths and showers can seem threatening as do cars, planes and heights. They can also fear other people, not wanting to be near or talk to them.

> I don't like being in the shower recess. I wait until I am feeling reasonably well during the day to have my shower. If I have it when I am feeling a little bit nervy I'll panic and want to get out.

> I had to stop having baths for several months because I became convinced that there were sharks under the water, and the bath itself made me feel claustrophobic. I also developed a phobia about all sorts of other things during this time – dogs, thunderstorms – just everything.

> I had a phobia about making calls and answering the phone. I didn't have the courage to pick the phone up. I pulled it out or took it off the hook.

> I hadn't been on benzos long before I became terrified to drive over a bridge. I couldn't sit upstairs at the theatre. I used to feel I would somehow be sucked over the edge. I'm completely okay again now. I never think about where I'm going to sit or drive and take delight in looking over the edge of cliffs just to prove I can do it.

RESTLESSNESS AND AGITATION

These irritating and disruptive symptoms affect almost everyone in withdrawal.

> I might have an article on my desk, some ironing, some dishes there, some polishing somewhere

else. I would run around from one thing to another, then I'd go out and water the garden, then I'd come back and vacuum the house. Eventually, by doing a little bit, all the time, on all of these things, they'd all get done. But sitting down and doing one thing through from beginning to end was just not possible. This is completely different from how I used to be; I was extremely methodical at doing one thing and sticking with it.

Somehow the ironing seemed to beckon me at about two in the morning. I couldn't sleep and I couldn't sit still to watch a bit of telly, so I did the ironing. It was the motion and the rhythm – it was soothing. It kept me moving and I didn't feel so restless. Before, I could sit still for hours on a couch, reading, or beside a river fishing.

One tell-tale sign of withdrawal is constant, restless body movement.

I can only go to the cinema or theatre if there is going to be a lot of action. I can't sit still. When I'm reading or watching TV, I get wriggly and restless and my concentration goes. I'm not at peace in my body yet. I get jumping legs which makes me want to jiggle, and then there is this winding foot action.

It is not just bodies which are restless in benzo withdrawal, it is minds as well. Thoughts seem to be on fast-forward. This can make working very difficult; people must quickly write their thoughts down, or else vital points are forgotten.

My mind speeds up and sometimes my mouth too. You have to try and make a conscious effort to slow down because once you get into anything, you do it in a real rush. When I try to do something that's technical it will take a long time to do properly. I find I mess up what I'm doing because I can't slow down and take it calmly.

The intense feelings of agitation in withdrawal seem to strike without reason, and are amplified by anxiety and stress. They can be very distressing.

It is definitely body chemistry that is doing it. It is the body that is agitated, not the mind. My brain isn't agitated. My body pumps adrenalin out for no apparent reason. It seems unrelated to anything which is happening at the time.

I find the agitation very distressing. It is an awful on-edge, nervy feeling. I can't concentrate at all when I have it. It is as if my whole being is on red-alert waiting for disaster to strike.

If you are sitting in a chair, relaxing, there is an anxiety, restlessness and agitation which is irrational, and it's something I did not have before taking pills. I believe that the physical symptoms come first and then the mind begins to worry. I find walking helps.

SECRETIONS

I had excessive saliva – I would be talking and my mouth would be bubbling copious saliva when I first came off – I used to think I was going to drown myself. My eyes watered constantly.

SEXUALITY

Some people find that withdrawal affects their level of sexual interest, swinging from none to too much. Desire can vanish completely – for months, even years. When people do have sex, out of love and consideration for their partners, or a need for intimacy, they often find that it is completely exhausting.

> I had no libido for months after coming off the pills. The major factor was loss of sensation; am I in or not, who could tell?

> I had sexual problems because of the energy needed. Sex gave me the same symptoms as if I'd been lifting weights – that ill, drained feeling.

At the other extreme is sexual obsession and grossly heightened sexual desire. Some people find that they are tormented by lust.

> Later in withdrawal I was randy as a rabbit, over the moon, crazy with it. One day I went down to the Moe races with my wife, and on the way back I could hardly keep the car on the road for randiness.

> I was in a state of sexual excitement a lot of the time. I thought about sex constantly; it was the only thing I thought about, I couldn't switch off

and watch the news or think about anything else.
The whole thing was ridiculous. I think if I was
experiencing a serious hormonal imbalance such
as an increased male hormone, this would explain
adequately the increase in sexual feeling.

Bizarre sexual thoughts and fantasies

Violent, disturbing sexual thoughts and fantasies
may occur, often about taboo subjects like incest,
child molestation or even bestiality. Such
thoughts are absolutely terrifying because they
arouse fears of going crazy or turning into a monster.

There is one terribly dark side to this libido thing –
I started to have the thoughts of a child molester.
You wouldn't do anything but you'd be feeling
horrible that you could even think like those men.
You felt like a real liability around children. If
there was a story about a child molester in the
paper I'd read it. It's a very weird sort of sexuality –
your mind is almost dragged screaming to these
horrific situations – you tend to go towards the
worst of everything. It's almost evil at times. Even
now sometimes my mind reverts back to it. My
coping device is to say, this is withdrawal, forget it.
Imagine going through this and not knowing what
was happening to you.

It is not only men who have such experiences;
women are just as badly affected.

I used to think about animals and things like that –
really weird. And same sex, doing it with women,

which is the last thing on my mind. And with kids! I felt disgusting! I'd never do anything, but that's the fear when you are thinking and feeling like that.

Often in bed I would be in a strange state suspended between waking and sleeping. This vile horror would start – it was somewhere between a dream and a vision. Rats or snakes or spiders would seem to plunge into my vagina and chew and bite it. I would be half awake at the time so I would try to throw off the vision but I couldn't – I had to let it run its course. It usually lasted a few minutes.

Another thing was a waking fantasy which would suddenly overcome me, sometimes in the middle of an ordinary day. I mean, imagine it – I'm a respectable middle-aged woman. I'd have to stop what I was doing and go and lie down on the bed while the fantasy played out. I would masturbate and that episode would be over. It was about father–daughter sex. I had a particular scenario that I would follow through, the same every time. I don't want to describe it. The fantasy would have me completely in its grip and I would give myself up to it.

I found this fantasy very alluring and that was partly what made the whole thing so horrible. These episodes started during the last year I was taking the pills and lasted for about two years after I came off them. I've never ever had such experiences before or since, so I have absolutely no doubt that they were caused by those tablets. I hate to think what would have happened if I had described these thoughts to a psychiatrist!

People feel very isolated by these terrible thoughts; they are often too embarrassed and afraid to talk about them. And for those who go through benzo withdrawal without knowing that such thoughts are a symptom, the worst fear is that they might act out their fantasies.

I met a man through a support network. Later he rang me and told me he was having these thoughts – he was even afraid to have his granddaughter on his knee. When I told him it was a withdrawal symptom he just cried.

When I heard or read about a person who did something like incest I was terrified that I might do it too. Not that I had an urge to do it, but that I hoped I didn't reach the stage where I could do it without wanting to. I think that when you're well and healthy and normal these things don't affect your subconscious mind, but I was in a low, weak state mentally. Those things would make an impression on me and I couldn't throw them off. Things that normally you wouldn't think about take over your mind.

SHAKING AND INNER TREMOR

Almost all those in withdrawal experience attacks of the shakes, often while still taking benzos. In fact, shaking or an unsettling inner tremor can be one of the first signs that something is wrong. When coming off the pills, both the shaking and the inner tremor can become very pronounced: some people can hardly hold a cup of tea without spilling it. The severe shaking usually settles down and becomes less visible after a few weeks – it's still there, but you can't see it.

The inner tremor seems to worry people for much longer. They find it disconcerting, especially when trying to sleep. Moving about a lot seems to help, even if it's just wriggling or shifting in your seat.

I started to get the shakes at work while I was still on Valium. It was so embarrassing – my hands and my head were shaking and I felt my mouth quivering too. When I came off, my whole body shook for days – I felt like I was going to shake to bits. Later I was left with an inner tremor which I had for several years, non-stop. That came and went in the last year or so and now I never have it unless I get extremely tired or something upsets me.

I had a lot of shaking. Awful inner shaking – it seemed that my heart and all the mechanics were shaking – I can still get that. It starts at the chest then radiates out until my whole body is involved. You can't see it. It is like what you see in a heat wave – that sort of heat shimmer. It is a physical thing for me, not an emotional thing.

SKIN

Skin colour and tone often change when people take benzos. Rashes, dry, flaky skin and itching are common as are sore spots, acne and hypersensitivity. People find it hard to tell whether objects are too hot or cold, and some rough items can feel smooth. These symptoms affect many people.

> For about eighteen months after I stopped the pills, I had a continual itchy rash all over my neck, shoulder and chest; very tiny spots, a bit like german measles, which, if I scratched them, would turn into blotches.

> A lot of dry patches of skin with flakiness. I came out in pimples all over my body, even in my hair. They left scars.

> I had sore spots on me. On my chest, arms and legs. There was no rash or bruise, just a sore spot on the skin.

> I had hypersensitivity all over my body – I was constantly feeling fretful and uncomfortable and irritable with it. I couldn't wear anything too tight.

SLEEP PROBLEMS

Some sleep disturbance seems very common, occurring sometimes for years after coming off benzos. It can be caused by withdrawal symptoms such as racing thoughts, headaches, muscle pain, breathing difficulties and panic attacks. But it is mostly withdrawal insomnia which keeps people awake. This may start while people are still on the pills, or can begin months after the last benzo is taken. It seems to be much worse for people who have been prescribed benzos for sleep difficulties.

> It was horrendous. I'm six years off pills and I'm still not sleeping well. For a year I hardly slept at all. Even the second year I wasn't much better. It was like having a railway station going through my mind, and that made me frantic. I was agitated and would go into a sort of peripheral kind of sleep and then I would wake up with the agitation again. I went to a sleep psychologist who thought that it was not a psychological problem. I can still have a night when I don't sleep at all.

> I was getting about eight hours' sleep before I started to come down, but then my sleep pattern started to go berserk. I had anything from four hours to one hour at times. The norm was about four or five hours of unbroken sleep – if I got that I thought I was doing well. Last month I have gone backwards. I don't know why – I've got no hassles.

> When I'm having a bad night it's like what I would imagine sleep deprivation caused by Russian Secret Police would be like.

Waking up in a panic worries a lot of sufferers. They can get off to sleep but know they will probably wake up with palpitations or a terrible start.

> I used to go off to sleep quite well, but once or twice during the night I would wake up with either palpitations or a panic attack. I would be terrified.

My heart would be going and I couldn't get my breath. I had it for a long time.

In the morning

Most people wake up feeling as if they haven't been to sleep and as though they have a bad hangover; they feel drugged, tired and sometimes depressed. Some feel so awful they wish they had not woken up at all.

There have been so many mornings I have opened my eyes and wished I were dead. I feel so ill, so depressed, and I very often snooze on and on, which in the end makes me feel worse.

When I wake up in the morning I feel very tired still. I have to kick-start myself. I have two or three cups of tea and I sit there for ages. If I have to get up and rush, I get palpitations. I was never like this before. I can't have a shower until much later as my heart starts going and I feel shaky.

I feel pretty bad when I wake up in the morning. It feels like there is all this poison in my system which is making me feel awful, physically and mentally. My muscles feel like they contain all this rubbish. I start slowly and feel better as I go along. I don't feel like talking – it feels like a rubber band that has been stretched to its limit.

'I'm always sleeping'

Sleep is a great healer and very often when people stop their pills they simply sleep on and off for days or months.

In the early days, especially the first two years, it was just sleep, sleep, sleep. It seemed like the body was just unwinding and trying to recover from all the pills, hence all the sleep. I was probably awake six hours out of twenty-four. For the first twelve months, I'd hurry to do the housework because I knew this dreadful feeling of tiredness would come over me and I'd absolutely have to lie down and go to sleep. I used to try and fight it but it was no use.

Daytime naps

It is almost impossible not to fall asleep during the day, especially if sleep has been only fitful the night before. Many people find it helps to have a nap – it keeps them going. Others loathe it – it makes them feel ghastly.

A late afternoon doze – just drifting off, quite delicious when I fell into it. But it took me into a bleak twilight land, like a bad fairy had put a spell on me. I would wake in shock, my body feeling vile. Toxic snoozes, I called them. It could take me hours to recover.

When I got home from work at five-thirty, I would crash for about an hour even though I felt agitated when I woke up. It was the only way I could keep going.

SOCIAL AND COMMUNICATION SKILLS

Communicating with others often becomes just too much effort for most people in withdrawal.

I opt out of conversations where I used to partici-
pate, and I say to myself, you're becoming like
your nan. When she got old it was as if she wasn't
there. We all used to love her but she didn't join in
the conversation – she sat back. I find I've been
like that in withdrawal – I've sat back because I
desperately want to be with people but I haven't
got the energy.

What makes matters worse is that socialising
can bring on other unpleasant symptoms such as
inner tremor and depersonalisation.

I can't keep talking. I have to pretend that I have
something else to do. If I keep going I just get more
and more tired and become depersonalised. The
person I'm talking to becomes blurry in front of me.

The effort of concentrating on a conversation for too
long would bring on a shaky, shuddery, trembly
feeling, and sometimes I'd start to feel cut off from
reality and the other person.

Because of poor memory and concentration,
people fear the embarrassment of losing track of
the conversation or saying the wrong thing. And
low self-esteem means that they feel they simply
have nothing worthwhile to say.

I'll wait for other people to talk because I'll say
something and it will be really stupid. When I
went to church this Sunday, a member of the
church council welcomed me. I had something
going around in my head that he'd said the week

before which I started to respond to as if he'd just said it. He wouldn't have known what I was talking about.

Because your self-esteem takes a battering your social skills do as well. I always thought of myself as a fairly extrovert happy-go-lucky sort of person who could mix in any company fairly readily, but on the pills I didn't do anything – I sat back and let things happen around me.

A minority of people suffer a strange conversational paralysis, experiencing episodes where they can't speak at all.

I used to call it 'The Silence'. I would write it in big capital letters in my diary. When it hit I'd be in a social situation – nothing too taxing, just with old friends – and find that I just couldn't bring myself to speak. It was like that comment our grannies used to make when we were out and didn't fulfil our social obligations – 'cat got your tongue?'

One time a dear friend from overseas was making a rare visit. I organised a little group to go out for dinner and then sat there all night without saying a single word. I'm normally very chatty, so my friend was bemused. She made kind efforts to bring me into the conversation, but eventually gave up. It might not sound like any great trauma, but it was very embarrassing. It seems incredible now that I'm back to my old self and the main problem is to get me to shut up, but I still wince whenever I think of that evening.

All of these factors can lead to social phobia. This is quite different from feeling a little antisocial; it is a real fear of being in company.

> People have been a real worry to me. I'd be quite happy to sit here and listen to music, go outside, drive the car somewhere – anywhere to be away from people.

> I haven't wanted to be with people. I can't be bothered putting in the extra effort. I can fool somebody for a period of time if I have to. I can't keep it up for long – if we have someone to dinner I'm pretty glad when they've gone. I wasn't like this before – I didn't want dinner parties to end. There's a hell of a difference now. Socially, I don't want to go out anywhere if I can help it, because I'm not sure of myself – I just want to be. I'm not living life like this.

Because of this lack of sociability, it can seem that a weird change of personality has occurred. Those who were once gregarious and outgoing start to avoid the social occasions they once enjoyed with family and friends. This is puzzling and upsetting for the other people involved, and can damage relationships in the long run.

> I used to tell my parents that if I was having a downer and someone came to visit I would go to my room and they were not to tell them that I was there. It was so bad that I didn't participate in any social activities for eighteen months. This is much better now, though it's not back to normal. Even

six months ago if I'd had to go and visit someone I'd have wanted to avoid it, but now I'm often looking for someone to visit.

STOMACH

Stomach symptoms such as pain, indigestion, bloating, rumbling and nausea trouble a lot of people.

I had bad stomach pain after I came off the pills – it was bad for months. I was vomiting when I first came off the pills and I had terrible pain, and no one knew what the problem was in the hospital – or they wouldn't say the symptoms were caused by the pills. I had a scan and all the tests they give you, and there was nothing. The pain was very severe, so bad that one weekend we called a locum who was more willing to say something about the withdrawal than any other doctor I have ever been to. He told me the symptoms I was experiencing were definitely caused by coming off the pills. I had bad indigestion too, for months. I lived on Mylanta.

Terrible gripey feelings under my ribs, the kind of feelings you get if you are terribly nervous or if you have eaten something acidic.

I got bad indigestion and some wind. I used to eat Quickeze – I sometimes ate two packets a day. I had a roiling, twisting sensation in my stomach, and a huge amount of rumbling. My wife was always commenting on the rumbling. It took a long time to go away.

Bloating – ten months pregnant. It comes and goes. I have really got a gut which I never used to have. I always eat light salads, never any fattening food, so my sense of it is that it is definitely connected with the pills.

I got bouts of the most horrible nausea, nothing like anything I have ever had before. I felt sort of toxic with it, radioactive, as though I'd glow in the dark. God, I hated it. It would last a couple of hours then vanish. Eventually it vanished for good.

STRANGE SENSATIONS AND ELECTRIC SHOCKS

Benzos can cause a variety of weird physical sensations. The most common are that ants are crawling over your arms and legs, or worms are moving under your skin. Hair may feel wet when it's dry. These sensations are often disturbing.

It felt as though I had things crawling over my skin for a long time. I would feel there was something there even when there wasn't – it happened a lot. There are mites you can't see with the naked eye and I thought perhaps I had become so sensitive I could feel them walking on me – seriously!

Electric shocks

There can be a feeling of electric tingling, or a shock right through the body, or just one arm or leg.

I had electric shocks right through my body for a long time. They were big jolts – you could see me move with them. I had a sort of tingly, zingy feeling too. I had it all the time for a while, then I used to get it only in the afternoons when I got tired.

SWEATING AND BODY TEMPERATURE

The body's internal thermostat often seems to go out of control in withdrawal. Temperature can fluctuate from very cold to very hot in a short space of time.

I never knew what temperature I was. I started withdrawal in autumn, and I'd head off in the morning wearing thermal underwear. By lunchtime it would be intolerable and I'd take it all off. By afternoon I'd be cold and put it all back on again. I think you're as sensitive to temperature as you are to everything else.

A sensation of burning, flushing heat is most common. People say that their body temperature seems to have mysteriously gone up several degrees. They may find themselves wearing light clothing and sleeping with fewer blankets, and they begin to dread the warmer weather.

When I was on the tablets my body temperature was very high, and even though I've come off them it still is. I don't know how I could sleep in a double bed with a girl because my body is so hot. I knocked the doona off my bed last night – it's only a two-blanket doona. It's not always like that – it comes and goes during the night. It has nothing to do with the outside temperature, or summer or winter. Sometimes I've been so hot I've hopped straight in the shower. People can feel it – blokes at work will grab me and say, 'God, you're hot.'

I had to dress very lightly. I very rarely wear woollen clothes even in winter whereas I used to love all my woolly sweaters and had a huge collection of them. Now I dress in layers of cotton clothes.

Profuse sweating often goes with this – including night sweats, particularly in early withdrawal. This is socially embarrassing as well as unpleasant.

Some mornings in winter I'd break into a sweat and I'd be sitting in front of the fan with my singlet on, dribbling with perspiration. It was horrible because it used to come with a depressed feeling.

TASTE

Eating can be spoiled in withdrawal because of the metallic taste in their mouths. They can't recognise flavours – many foods do not taste the same and it is hard to tell whether the foods are sweet or sour.

I had a metallic taste for the first few years. It tasted like I had chomped on the bumper bar of an old Chrysler car.

I experienced the strangest taste; it was an antiseptic flavour. I had it quite often, as well as other unusual tastes – they varied a bit, so at least that was interesting.

TEETH AND GUMS

A number of people experience sore teeth, more like neuralgia than toothache. Their teeth feel loose in their sockets and are very sensitive to hot and cold. Sore, bleeding gums are common.

> I am still having problems with my teeth. I had very sensitive aching teeth and was referred to a crown-and-bridge dentist who gave me a new occlusion which cost many thousands of dollars, but did not fix the problem. Often my teeth don't feel solid or hard any more; they feel like rubber – a really weird sensation. I still grind my teeth at night which I had never done before I took Valium.

> I found myself covering my mouth with my hand. My gums looked puffy for months. Nearly every time I brushed my teeth, my gums would bleed. I was doing all the right things – using dental floss and rubbing my gums but nothing helped and then one day they stopped bleeding. I hadn't changed my diet or cleaned my teeth in a different way, so it was hard to fathom. Now they're fine – pink and healthy.

THROAT

Throat symptoms affect only a few people. For those who do suffer, the most common problem is a recurring mild sore throat. 'Gunky' throats which have to be cleared all the time with an 'er-hem' sort of cough are also experienced. Throat pain and ulcers take the joy out of eating. Repeated dry, scratchy throats make people think they have developed allergies. The most worrying symptom is a sensation of choking – people panic when they feel they cannot swallow.

> I would get halfway through a swallow and I couldn't complete it; I thought I would choke. I looked like one of those turkey gobblers because I developed a head-bobbing action when I was trying to encourage the food to go down. My muscles seem to go into spasm. It sometimes felt like someone was trying to strangle me. I also had a nasty pain in my throat – like it was badly bruised. The trouble was, I had a horror of it. I was terrified that it was life-threatening – like it could be cancer.

> I had mild sore throats and throat ulcers, one after the other, which never seemed to develop into anything worse. It went on for ages. My friends wondered what was wrong with me, as I explained yet again that my throat was just a bit sore.

UNREALITY AND DEPERSONALISATION

Depersonalisation makes people feel their bodies and often their personalities are unreal, physically outside themselves as well as disconnected emotionally. They can seem non-human, like a cog in a machine. People sometimes feel like two separate individuals. Sensations of unreality are very common and can start very soon after taking benzodiazepines.

I thought I was two people, one telling the other what to do. As if some of me is here and another me is doing something else. I used to get it really badly for a long time after I came off benzos, but I hardly ever get it now.

At times I had a feeling of floating in and out of myself. I seemed to be looking down and watching things happening to me. I didn't feel centred, and there was a feeling of voyeurism – like two people with one operating a puppet. There was no choice involved – it just happened. I felt like this while on pills and for a long time afterwards, years. Those feelings have mostly gone but there are times when I can slip away; mainly when I am very tired or stressed or if I concentrate for too long.

'I'm not really here'

People have the impression that they are not there at times. They feel ghost-like, as though they don't have a body. When this happens, their emotional responses become alien to them. Sometimes they look at themselves in the mirror and can't quite recognise themselves.

I lost my sense of self; it wasn't me thinking or talking – it freaked me right out, as though someone could look at you and not see you.

I often feel that I'm not me, that I'm looking at somebody else – that what is happening is not actually happening to me. I can see her but she can't see me; it's like looking at a film of yourself or hearing your voice on tape, and thinking, that's not me. I'm really out of myself . . . some actor is playing me.

There were times when I was not sure on which side of the mirror I was standing – like a kitten darting behind the mirror looking for itself. I wafted in and out of myself for years and found it almost impossible to talk to people. If you don't quite know who you are it is impossible to relate to others – you have no frame of reference.

Feeling unreal in familiar surroundings – for example, walking into your home and thinking it does not look like your home, is called de-realisation.

I found it hard to believe that the things around me were real too. Other people seemed strange, familiar shops looked somehow different, everything felt wrong.

Cut off
Being detached, feeling separated or isolated as though in a fog is very alarming.

I felt a part of me had left and walked out the door. I had that feeling soon after I started taking benzodiazepines, like I'm inside a glass jar, looking out; like there is something between me and the world and everything looks a little bit different. When I get tired it gets worse and the glass of the jar gets thicker and thicker. At other times things look a bit hazy, like a mist in between, separating me from the world.

Losing touch

When people feel depersonalised they become alienated from others, making it hard to go to work or spend an evening with friends.

> Unless you have experienced being detached it is difficult to imagine it – the sadness, the utter despair of reaching out and not being able to connect with another person, and even worse, not wanting to try any more because the real you has gone. I never valued the close, warm feelings you have with others before I lost them – I never thought about them – they were just there. Nothing seems to help this condition – it has to run its course and eventually it goes away.

> Losing touch devastated me. I remember beginning to feel unreal soon after I started taking Ativan and I found doing interviews at work more difficult as I became more and more out of touch with myself and my surroundings. When I stopped taking Ativan, I became much worse. Talking to friends was hard and family life was disrupted as I withdrew more and more into myself. It had something to do with three-dimensional perception. I couldn't see myself any more as a three-dimensional person – I had no sort of inner picture or idea of myself, that just disappeared. It slowly wore off after a couple of years and I returned to my family and friends.

VOICE AND SPEECH

Problems with voice and speech affect only a few people in withdrawal. Those who do experience symptoms find that the quality of their voices seems to change. From sounding clear and strong, it can become hoarse, weak and trembly.

> The only place I felt comfortable speaking was at a support group meeting where no one commented on my wavering voice – there were always others who sounded the same.

> For a long time after I came off benzos my voice had all the colour and emphasis drained out of it. I spoke in a flat monotone like a robot. My voice was weak – I could only turn up the volume to about three, whereas normally I would be able to turn it up to ten. I can really roar quite loudly now, after four years off the pills. I love being able to use my voice again, speaking out aloud to a group of people, having a sense of using my voice as an instrument.

Speaking can become humiliating for people when they come off pills. They never know when the words are going to be lost. It isn't mental confusion, they know what they want to say but they can't get the words out.

> My mouth and brain were both working okay. But for some time I didn't seem to have access to my thoughts. It was like the telephone lines were down. The information was organised and ready to go, but the equipment was faulty.

> I could think of what I wanted to say, but I couldn't get it out. I went to the local shop one

day where I met a friend who was a football supporter, but I couldn't discuss the football even though I knew a lot about it. I could see my friend looking at me oddly. This problem lasted for a long time but has lessened over the last six to eight months.

Such pauses and blocks in conversation are embarrassing, making people nervous in social situations.

I was like Billy Budd in the film. He was a handsome sailor and he became inarticulate in moments of stress. When he was accused of being a mutineer he found it impossible to speak, so he hit the officer who said it. So he really did become a mutineer. I call this the Billy Budd syndrome – you have quite clear and elaborate thoughts that just don't get articulated. A lot of the time I would say, what's the use, or tell myself that I'm too tired to be putting out all the time, but mostly it was just a mystery that was happening and went on happening. There was nothing in me that would let me fight it or do anything about it. It was a constant in the earlier days when I was tired and exhausted all the time. I don't experience this now.

When I tried to say something it was as if there was an 'entity' that had control over what I said, so there were certain things I just couldn't get out, couldn't say. This 'entity' was in my neck – again, I know that sounds strange, but it felt that way. It felt like some kind of electrical activity – like an interference in my neck, and then I couldn't speak. It was really severe and made worse by the fear of not knowing what was wrong with me. My speech has a slightly hesitant quality now but I can talk almost as fluently as I did before.

Part IV

....

What Helps
and What Doesn't

What Helps

The only known cure for benzo illness is time. Time for the brain to start working again and time for the body to heal. In spite of this, people try to find ways to feel better. And there is no shortage of advice and therapies available. They try just about everything: aromatherapy, bach flower remedies, acupuncture, homoeopathy, bio-feedback, kinesiology, primal therapy, psychotherapy and drama, counselling, massage, relaxation, meditation, and exercise programs. These remedies can cost a lot too; and what is good for one person is not necessarily good for another. The cheapest and most old-fashioned remedies are still the best: information, support, good diet and rest. Acceptance and motivation lead to recovery too.

Information

Accurate information about benzo illness is found to be extremely beneficial to recovery. It makes sense that if you understand what to expect, you are much more able to deal with the fear, pain and ongoing symptoms. Any information about how to cope with withdrawal is eagerly sought and swapped with other benzo sufferers. Magazine articles and books about other people's experiences are read and re-read. And if you are too sick to read, tapes explaining how to deal with the illness are often the answer.

> Reading about what happened to other people helped me the most. I could relate to that because I felt the same way. I read every piece of literature I could find on the subject. There was one book I read so often it fell to bits, and I had to buy another copy. Television and radio were great. I was always in awe of the people who agreed to go on radio or TV when they were extremely sick. They were so determined to let others know what had happened to them.

Support

Sufferers have to keep living their lives and it helps if there are supportive people around. Maybe a boss who can reschedule some of the workload, or a friend who can look after the kids for a while. A confidante to listen, offer some advice or maybe just to be there, so you can feel safe. And if people are very ill, someone to care for them. Adequate support is essential to help people recover.

> Number one is my husband. I could not have coped without him. I think that I would have gone back on to pills. Occasionally I found someone who helped me and encouraged me. One was a dietitian who knew about withdrawal and she told

me how wonderful I was to do it. I have a lovely friend who is very happy and she makes me laugh and I like to be with her – she is a great comfort to me. I have another friend who really understands what I am going through and she asks me how I am, and that is a great comfort also. I can relax with both of these friends.

Good food

A well-balanced diet is what most people find helpful in withdrawal – low in fat, high in complex carbohydrates and dietary fibre, and moderate in protein. Because people often have such low energy levels and extreme lethargy, they are constantly drawn to refined and sugar-rich foods – it gives an instant energy lift. But they find the short-term effects are not worth it. The let-down that follows makes their depression and lethargy worse. Soft drinks, artificial flavourings, preservatives, and stimulants such as tea, coffee and cola drinks have the same effect.

The craving for sugar in withdrawal can be very powerful. I used to try to stay on a sugar-free diet because eating refined food and sugar made me feel worse in the long run. But I nearly always failed. I seemed to be on a roller-coaster ride of mood changes and sugar binges. I tried not to keep sweet things in the house.

It was several years before I could balance my diet sensibly and even then I would break out. I would suddenly get in the car and drive to the nearest shop where I could get a sugar hit.

People have noticed that blood-sugar levels seem to go haywire in withdrawal. This can cause dizziness, tremor, feelings of panic and disorientation. They find that eating small meals regularly is the best – no over-eating or bingeing. Instead of reaching for a cake or lolly, a few almonds or a cold potato are favourite pick-me-ups.

> I try to eat every couple of hours because I find I become nervous if I don't. It's like hypoglycaemia – a drop in the blood sugar. I eat a wholewheat biscuit or a tomato or some salmon. Sometimes I get up in the middle of the night and have some milk and breakfast cereal. It's soothing food and it helps. All the carbohydrate foods take away the nervous feeling.

A lot of people feel they have been poisoned by benzos and that the plainest, purest food is what they need. Fresh organic fruit and vegetables, purified water and no preservatives or food colourings are favoured to help the body detoxify. Some become vegetarian and feel better for that; others have the opposite experience and feel they need meat to give them energy. They discover that anti-candida diets are helpful too. Most book-shops carry a wide selection of titles on vegetarian cooking, and hypoglycaemia and anti-candida diets.

Rest

Adequate rest is essential in recovery. Lying on a bed or couch, watching a video or listening to the radio, is often the best medicine. People spend weeks, months, and in a few cases years doing virtually nothing apart from a little gentle exercise: 'At first, all I could do was rest. I did the housework, a little bit at a time, often not finishing a job until later in the day.' As people improve it is important for them to have balance in their lives – too much work or play exhausts them. They learn to recognise the signs, and rest. If not, some of the old symptoms come back. They know they have to 'wait it out', to be patient.

Acceptance and motivation

One of the most difficult things in withdrawal is learning to accept that you may have a long-term illness. But people discover that staying angry about what benzos have done to them does not help – it gets in the way of recovery. There are enough problems dealing with the extra anger caused by benzos without adding to it. Once they have understood what to expect, positive thinking and self-talk is a good way to help change mindsets. If used effectively, they can motivate and change negative attitudes. As soon as the old hurts or destructive and frightening thoughts appear, people find that if they change them immediately into more constructive thoughts and actions, they can change. Especially if practised each day.

> I believe you can change things. Not in the bad stages of withdrawal when you have acute symptoms. But when you get a little bit better. I overcame agoraphobia by forcing myself to go out and using positive self-talk.

Acceptance is a big thing. To tell yourself to accept and float – not fighting the symptoms helped me a lot. Saying to yourself that these are just funny feelings, you are okay, you are not going to faint, you are not going to die, the feelings won't hurt you – it is just fear.

What Might Help
Support groups and therapies

The following treatments and therapies were beneficial to some people while others found them useless and even harmful. For some, even if the treatment is costly and even if there is not much improvement, at least they feel they have tried something – they are making an effort to get better.

One-to-one and telephone counselling
Talking regularly to a professional counsellor who understands benzo withdrawal is considered one of the most helpful ways to recovery. People often like to go to the same person to make a connection, as they feel very vulnerable when they come off benzos. They may need to go over the same ground, with the same thought or symptom. This behaviour can be exhausting for friends, but it is often part of the recovery process.

Sexual problems and frightening thoughts are also hard to talk about, and for some it is much easier to confront these fears in a one-to-one therapy session.

Personal counselling was a vital part of my recovery. For the first twelve months I was very confused, and so many different things were happening to me. That is why it was good to go to just one particular person as they understood what I was going through. And you may not feel happy talking in a group situation about some of the things you are feeling. The sexual bit is very important. These are very personal things.

The most important thing for me was counselling. The fact that I was feeling so ill all the time was really worrying me and reassurance was excellent. That there was someone who understood what was wrong, and kept telling me that there was a light at the end of the tunnel – I needed that optimism. I found that some medical people could not understand what was wrong with me – they didn't know, and didn't believe me.

Withdrawal symptoms like depression and phobias can be wrongly diagnosed as mental illness and inappropriately treated. Consequently, the advice given is often wrong and of little comfort or support. 'The counselling I received was inadequate because it made me feel I should be pulling my socks up – they seemed judgemental.' Also, many people think that the ability to cope with stressful situations is masked when taking benzos: 'The pills do the job for you.' So, after coming off the pills, there seems to be a long period when they are particularly vulnerable to pressure. Very often, this is not recognised. An experienced counsellor who fully understands withdrawal is needed for those who have to learn new skills to cope with stress.

> I went to a psychologist for a while but found that she didn't know the first thing about withdrawal, so I stopped going to her. You really need someone who knows about withdrawal to help you understand the symptoms and what you are going through. I don't think psychological counselling is appropriate in the early stages. Some people would need psychological counselling later on when they could think straight.

> I found an unconventional psychiatrist – I couldn't have done without him. He greeted me with a big hug. You can go to family and friends for just so long. You need the emotional support of one-to-one therapy, it's vital. He taught me breathing methods which lead to the healing of pain and unpleasant emotions.

There is often a need to talk to someone immediately – a sudden attack of panic, a new symptom or just the ongoing awfulness of withdrawal, can make people frightened or despairing. Some are too ill to leave their homes or cannot afford fares or counselling. Being able to pick up the phone and call a counsellor adds some security to those who feel isolated by withdrawal symptoms. Even those with phone-phobias seem to be able to overcome their fear because the reassurance is more important.

Support groups

Being able to talk about experiences, swap symptoms with others who are going through withdrawal, is rated one of the most helpful forms of support. Even if you are too ill or too anxious to talk, listening allows you to understand your symptoms better and helps you realise you are not alone. Some people find they can't sit still and have to walk around the room; some need to cry a lot, and others just sit and shake. All this is perfectly okay. Everyone there understands and sympathises. Unfortunately, there are some who can no longer drive or are too agoraphobic to go to support groups. But often, after a few months, the symptoms improve and they find they can get there occasionally. For those people especially, swapping telephone numbers so that they can support each other is one of the best solutions to loneliness and fear.

> I liked having a cross-section of people to talk to, so I don't think individual counselling would have been as good for me. I liked the reassurance from many people – it was a comfort.

> The people in the support groups were the ones who had lived it, they could tell me that I was not going mad and that the symptoms I had were the same as they had experienced. If people go to the meetings they will hear their symptoms discussed and even if they are too shy or ill to talk, they will eventually hear what they need to know.

Relaxation and meditation

There is an enormous amount of faith and hope invested in relaxation and meditation therapies because they seem so healthy and natural – which makes them particularly appealing to people who are trying to detoxify. These techniques are warmly recommended by most health professionals treating people in benzodiazepine withdrawal. But are they always helpful in every case?

The potential health benefits of relaxation and meditation are now well known: lower blood pressure, decreased heart rate, slower breathing, increased ability to handle stress. Many people practise some form of relaxation or meditation throughout all or part of their withdrawal. They swear by it – it was the main thing that got them through.

> I did relaxation and found it enabled me to put any symptoms I was having aside for that period of time. Even if I had a headache I would still try and do the relaxation. It might not have been as successful as if I was doing it symptom-free, but it built up reserves of a calmness in me if I did it daily. It tops you up, so that if you have the free-floating anxiety or the headaches, it sees you through. Because of the relaxation I could make myself relax when I was having the free-floating anxiety. It wouldn't build. You know how fear will build until it gets to the point where you have to get up and do something to stop the panic? Well, the relaxation allows you to just let it pass.

> I got to the stage where it was very easy for me to just relax my whole body. When you're not having

symptoms as well as when you are having symptoms, you have to remind yourself to relax every
hour. Once an hour I would tell myself to relax and
take twenty deep breaths. Because you don't
realise how tight your body gets during the day you
find that by five o'clock you could be very tense.

However – successful as they are for many
people – it must be clearly stated that these techniques do not always work for everyone. In some
cases they even make matters worse. Some
people in robust good health find relaxation techniques hard to master. It is not surprising then
that people in withdrawal should have problems.
Other symptoms can get in the way of efforts to
practise the techniques correctly. For example,
relaxation – which is supposed to be effortless
and floating – often requires focus and concentration, and is very difficult for most people in withdrawal. In fact it can make them quite ill.

The relaxation method which requires clench-
ing and unclenching muscle groups should be
avoided – it is apt to bring on acute muscle
spasm. Some people even express a dread of their
relaxation – they are afraid that it is taking them
somewhere frightening, that they are 'sinking too
far'. Strange as it seems, the relaxation sessions
make them more anxious, especially when first
coming off the pills.

When my withdrawal anxiety got totally out of
hand I sought help from various different therapists including psychiatrists, counsellors and
naturopaths. Without exception all these folk rec-

ommended relaxation or meditation – to be honest I was never quite sure of the difference. They taught me their own methods. In some cases they had made their relaxation tapes which they sold me. The problem was that every time I tried any form of relaxation or meditation it seemed to make me really tense and shaky. Looking intently inward, disciplining myself to be mentally and physically still, focusing my mind on a single image – it just made my head hurt. I would come out of it with a jolt and my nerves would be more jangled than before. This made me feel a failure – if everyone else thought relaxation was so fantastic then why couldn't I do it?

Of course, for ages I blamed myself. I think I could do it now and get a lot out of it, and maybe I will try it again. The funny thing is, though, that now I am calm most of the time I don't really feel a need for relaxation exercises.

With relaxation it is like when a room is silent: you hear all the sound in the room, and when you try to sit very still and you have an inner tremor, you feel that tremor even more and it makes you more anxious.

One woman who was going through benzo withdrawal was actually working as a relaxation teacher at the same time – and even she found it hard to practise what she preached.

I did relaxation because I was giving the lessons. But I couldn't lie down and receive them myself for a couple of years. I'm always surprised that people could actually lie there completely still, because I certainly couldn't. If I tried I was worse off at the end of the session – my mind and body could not keep still.

People are often experiencing high levels of agitation and anxiety in withdrawal, so I now conduct my sessions on a one-to-one basis. People can choose to lie or sit, and are invited to change positions or even move about if they are uncomfortable. The relaxation process has really begun because of this sense of freedom and participation. Some find it hard to do longer relaxation sessions – relaxing for a shorter time can be preferable. People may be stressed at the prospect of 'letting go', but usually in a session, if only briefly, most are able to relax to some extent – almost by default. And that bit of success lifts their confidence, which is very important, as confidence can be so low in withdrawal. Sometimes people have a successful session and sometimes they don't, but this is not peculiar to benzodiazepine withdrawal, it's like that with anxiety in general. People say, 'Somehow I just couldn't let go tonight.'

Deep-breathing techniques are often taught as a companion to relaxation. They were found to be particularly useful as they can be done almost anywhere once you get the hang of it: 'There were so many times when twenty slow deep breaths got me through.' But deep breathing must be done correctly – if not it can make people feel ill as there is a tendency to over-breathe. Hyperventilation and erratic breathing can cause a number of unpleasant symptoms such as light-headedness, chest pains, panic, tingling and palpitations.

Under supervision, deep breathing can be effectively learnt if properly taught and practised a few times, and some find it easier to master than relaxation or meditation. Like sleep, relaxation can be elusive – the more you try to chase it, the farther off it seems to be. Because of this, other more natural and unstructured activities often prove just as beneficial as formal relaxation exercises: knitting, listening to music, reading, or sitting in the garden just letting the mind drift while listening to the birds.

Exercise

Vigorous exercise is usually assumed to be good for almost everyone. Lifestyle and fitness campaigns constantly urge us to become more active – and benzo people are no exception. Some hospital detox programs include arduous aerobics regimens that are a nightmare for patients who can barely lift themselves out of a chair. People who have been through withdrawal emphasise that when planning any exercise program the key phrase is 'take it easy'. By far the most beneficial form of exercise is gentle walking – going for a stroll.

> I walked miles and miles, slowly ambling along. It was the answer for me because anything more strenuous than walking made my symptoms much worse. I was so agitated I needed to move all the time. I liked to look at other people doing things in their gardens and around their houses. I believe that my body was moving helped to work off the chemicals in my system. It was physical relief and mental release.

One woman even found walking helpful when she was feeling at her most exhausted.

> When I have a spell of extreme lethargy I try to go for a walk. I do my deep breathing and notice my surroundings: the colours of the leaves, the trees, the sky. By the time I get back from my walk the exhausted feeling has gone. I try to be aware of the world around me rather than retreat into my exhaustion. Notice the creek, the different greens of the trees, the different shapes of the clouds. To anyone embarking on the withdrawal I'd say 'walk'. You can walk off your mania. I walked in all weathers.

Even walking around the house or garden was found to be beneficial: 'It did me good just to move my body from the loungeroom out to the yard and back a few times.' Gentle cycling too can be useful in the early days – although it is best to keep well away from busy streets! It helps to overcome agoraphobia, and the rhythms of pedalling promote calm. Milder exercise programs such as Tai Chi and yoga were all found to be helpful.

> I find yoga excellent. Sometimes it makes my back and muscles ache, but I do love it and it has a very calming effect on me. It also gives me the feeling that I am doing something positive. I have done yoga for about ten or twelve years and I did a lot in early withdrawal. I try not to expect too much of myself with it, and I go at my own pace. I use tapes and you can get books on it. It worked in early

withdrawal because in yoga you are doing something, whereas with relaxation I found it very hard to lie down and be still. If you do a series of yoga exercises before you try to do relaxation you will relax much better, you have stretched all your body and you are ready to lie down.

Massage

Massage is a form of touch therapy used to relax tense muscles. It would seem to be ideal for people in benzo withdrawal who have severe muscle problems. But experience shows that massage, too, should be approached with some caution. Deep, thorough massage, particularly in the early stages of recovery, was found by many to be painful and disturbing. One man nearly fainted after a particularly vigorous massage. Another sufferer could not drive her car home after a massage, so much did it stir up and intensify her symptoms.

> I tried to have massage once and it was a terrible experience – I felt as if a nerve had been activated and I screamed out and became agitated and had palpitations. I never went back.

Most people agree that gentle light massage is best; it can provide great comfort for fragile bodies in recovery. A masseuse who has been working with people in benzo withdrawal for many years advises that, foremost, massage should be enjoyable. Sometimes those in withdrawal are not relaxed enough to lie down on a massage table, in which case she has them sit in a chair, and massages neck and shoulders, hands and feet. If people are really uncomfortable she begins with the hands. As they begin to relax, she goes on to head and shoulders, always checking and asking the client to let her know if it gets too much. After years of benzo use, muscles have been over-relaxed. Gentle massage stimulates the muscles and helps remove toxins – all of which is very important in recovery.

Acupuncture

Acupuncture is a Chinese technique which involves obtaining relief by inserting needles into pressure points on the body. Although it was helpful to some people, many others who tried it found it could bring on an acute bout of symptoms. One woman who was feeling well before her appointment had a severe panic attack after her acupuncture treatment. Another was plunged into a bout of crippling anxiety which lasted two months.

> I wouldn't recommend acupuncture, although it was good to start with. I felt in the end it was stirring up something. After a few treatments I felt that the activity was just going crazy in my head.

Overall, acupuncture was found to be unhelpful – even dangerous, as the following experience shows.

> After an acupuncture treatment I passed out while driving and ran into the car ahead of me. I was terrified. I never went back.

Other therapies

Homoeopathy, kinesiology, Chinese medicine, herbal remedies, naturopathy, aromatherapy and primal therapy are often tried with varying degrees of success. Many people rated the therapies very helpful; others tried most things on the menu but found none of them had much impact. There were indirect benefits, though. The ambience of alternative therapy clinics is often less frightening than a traditional doctor's surgery, and many people found it good to have somewhere pleasant to go when they were feeling sick and weak. The practitioners of these therapies were often found to be caring and ready to listen.

> I tried kinesio-therapy and homoeopathy. Neither of them produced startling results but they helped by providing a focus for treatment and care. At least the practitioners took withdrawal seriously and also the problems created by benzos. Trouble is that the drug affects so many organs and withdrawal seems to leap from one part of the body to another – so treatment is long and expensive.

This factor – the cost – causes many people to baulk at these therapies: 'I've spent thousands of dollars on this recovery. I've been to hypnotherapists, masseurs, acupuncturists, counsellors. About $4000 in three years.' Most alternative treatments are not rebatable on Medicare. And there is no hard evidence that any of them provide a miracle cure for withdrawal. People on a limited income often feel angry and cheated at having spent large sums of money on treatments and potions that have no noticeable effect on their illness. But for those who can afford them, such therapies can be reassuring and comforting – even if only because they give a vital sense of 'doing something'.

Things That Comfort

My garden is a comfort to me. I have a herb garden and bird feeders and I love watching the birds. In the darker days of withdrawal it was a great comfort to sit quietly watching the birds.

Warmth was a comfort to me – warm drinks, warm baths, warm showers, hotwater bottles and an electric blanket. Sunbathing helped and reading light novels – romance and historical novels – that take you out of yourself but don't exhaust you, because it is so hard to concentrate in withdrawal. Magazines were good too – *Nature and Health* was good because it described all sorts of natural therapies.

TV and videos were good too. The best things on TV were British comedies. I think that humour and laughter helps. The main thing is to take your mind off your symptoms. I believe that laughter and crying create and release the same endorphins that exercise releases. I find that if I have a really good cry I feel much better afterwards, I can feel it releasing the tension in me. I watched a lot of soaps on TV. Now that I can do more I don't watch them very much. I think that doing a course of study is a great comfort, too, not anything too hard, but something to take your mind off the withdrawal. I also found religion a comfort.

I used to ride my bike and turn my radio on and I loved that. It really relaxed me. I used to drift around the streets. When I was on benzos music didn't relax me but it does now. I like pop music. It was especially good after it rained; for about half an hour I would feel normal.

I liked to go to the movies. Sometimes just being on my own for a while helped.

Reading – not heavy, but good literature, and theology and beautiful writing, also the newspaper.

Puzzles – crosswords and other.

Listening to music – mainly classical.

Drives in the countryside. I feel that, had I been able, walks in the bush would have been a benefit.

Writing down special thoughts, philosophies, theologies, insights, as they have come to me.

Talking, talking, talking with my wife. An especial comfort to have one person who can 'take it' as it is. But I have to beware of transferring the 'black cloud' to her.

I've come to realise that beauty of any kind has comforted, supported and encouraged me in withdrawal – beautiful scenery, art, music, literature, architecture, furniture, textures, flowers – anything that is (to me!) a delight to the senses. The opposite is also true. Sickness, emptiness and ugliness pull me down.

My diary was my biggest comfort. In withdrawal you lose sight of how much you achieve and you also lose sight of what you have gone through to get where you are on that particular day. My diary gave me a permanent reminder of where I was when I started, where I was when I was having a bit of strife, and all the things I'd achieved in the middle.

I liked doing fancy work, cushions, to distract myself from symptoms.

Being with friends. Losing myself in movies or books. Massage, and having my hair done – those sorts of body things. Humour was terribly important – it was the only thing left, and I came to the conclusion that it must belong to a different part of the brain. Humour was the one thing that survived – you could always have a laugh.

Nature documentaries on TV helped – they are so peaceful and they don't expect anything of you – you don't have to think. Nature is very healing and soothing. Nature is very necessary.

Later on as my creativity started to return I started to do drawings of the withdrawal. This also helped.

Television and videos as a complete soporific. They make no demands, you only have to use your eyes to look at it. I watched a fair bit of trash, I suppose, anything that did not make mental demands.

I did a lot of tatting and found that terribly calming. It was good for your ego because you'd be tatting in the train and people would come up and say, 'Oh my mother used to do that', and your chest would fill up and you'd feel quite good. I think that's what you need, things to bring up your self-esteem.

Nothing much at all, not in the early stages. Then later, maybe lying in the bath helped a bit. I listened to the radio at night when I couldn't sleep. I could listen to talk-back but not to music. I loved music and now I love it again, but during withdrawal I couldn't listen to it at all. My daughter being here was a comfort to me.

I did a lot of knitting although I couldn't do pattern knitting.

Keeping going with playing the organ and with my painting. My faith was very important to me. I'm a Christian and I asked for anointing and the laying on of hands. After that I slept very well. It gave me confidence that I was going to recover. Prayer has helped me very much.

What Doesn't Help

Stress of any kind – particularly rushing, running late, being kept waiting or keeping someone else waiting. Even 'good' stresses can be a problem, like enjoying myself too much, being overcome by great scenery, a sunset, grandeur.

Sickness, emptiness and ugliness pull me down.

Trying to do too much on any one day.

Getting tired.

Disagreements and tensions between people.

The smell of dry-cleaned clothes, lacquers, paint, petrol.

Caffeine, sweet things, flavourings and food additives.

Too much (any!) poor quality food.

Bright sunlight and glare.

Loud crashing noise.

Sudden shocks like someone coming up behind me to surprise me.

Unfinished business – a book that has to be read, a room that needs to be tidied, accounts that need to be paid or letters to be written.

And then there are times I have avoided all of the exacerbating things but withdrawal has still been there just lurking round the corner. It has often pounced even when I've been taking good care of myself.

I feel as if my nervous system has been very badly damaged and if I do too much and get over-tired or if I have too much stress or a fight with one of the children, it brings on an attack of withdrawal. First I get very tired, a strange exhausted sort of tiredness, and then I get a light-headed feeling and maybe sinus pain, and then I become disconnected and depersonalised. It happens the same way each time.

Laughter accentuated the withdrawal symptoms. You cannot laugh or cry too much – anything that you do which uses too much emotion taxes your nervous system and makes you feel worse. The excitement of watching a horse-race would accentuate the symptoms. Sad thoughts are even more depressing. You have to stay calm and it is very difficult because it doesn't take much to upset you.

I think smoking is a disaster in withdrawal. The agitation makes you smoke more and it is another chemical going into your already overloaded system.

Alcohol and marijuana make my symptoms worse. Some exercise makes it worse and too many late nights. Night shift at work makes it hard.

If I go shopping I have to sit down after an hour and rest. If I don't, I get both emotionally and physically tired and the feeling of depersonalisation comes back. Sometimes I feel as though I am hypoglycaemic – tired and shaky.

Talking to people, especially if you don't get along with them too well, can be extremely exhausting.

I cannot stand the turmoil of rushing in the morning – it brings on the symptoms. I like to sit and collect my thoughts for a while. If somebody intrudes on that time I get upset and angry.

The symptoms were always much worse just before my period. Dental anaesthetics seemed to bring on a bad bout too.

I never let myself get too tired, too hungry or too thirsty.

A Note for Carers

To care for someone who is experiencing a severe and protracted withdrawal from benzodiazepines takes a lot of resilience, patience and compassion. Carers need to be fully informed and understand the unpredictability of the symptoms. That is, one day sufferers may be so ill they can't get up, and the very next day they are smiling and suggesting a walk. Sometimes a carer needs to be aware of the person's limits and try to gently guide them on a wiser course when they try to take on too much. It is important for carers not to be thrown when loved ones behave in a way which is hurtful and potentially damaging, but to see it as a probable effect of the benzodiazepines and not take it to heart.

Carers can become isolated, needing help and support themselves as they are very often stretched to the limit. It is perfectly normal for them to feel frustrated, resentful and angry about their situation. They often experience guilt when expressing any of these sentiments because they can see how the other person is suffering. Many carers find that counselling and time to themselves helps enormously. 'I need to get away sometimes. I feel if I have to hear the same symptoms one more time I'll scream. When it goes on for such a long time you begin to wonder whether you can take it.'

Benzos and Driving

'Warning: this medicine may cause drowsiness and may increase the effects of alcohol. If affected do not drive a vehicle or use machinery.'

This is the warning which now must be placed on the packaging of all benzodiazepines to comply with government regulations. Given the severity of the drug's side-effects and withdrawal symptoms, these warnings are weak and inadequate. People on benzodiazepines should not drink alcohol at all.

It has recently been recognised that benzodiazepines are the cause of many road accidents, especially when combined with alcohol. But what is still not fully understood is the degree of impairment that affects many people after they come off their pills, so much so that driving can be difficult or even impossible for months, sometimes years.

Benzo sufferers find that anxiety and panic attacks are common while driving, particularly on freeways, in heavy traffic, or a long way from home. Panic attacks while stopped at red lights are widely reported.

For years I dreaded driving. I hated the sense of the heavy bodies hurtling past me – the cars coming up in your rear-vision mirror. I used to stop if someone was tailgating me, or I'd just pull up out of sheer anxiety. I'd stop the car and wipe my hands on my jeans and walk about a bit, and then continue.

Perception and motor skills are badly affected. Sufferers find it hard to co-ordinate their hands and feet, and, most dangerous of all, make wrong decisions about overtaking other vehicles. 'If I were in the car with my husband I'd ask him whether he thought it was safe to pass. From being a skilful, assertive driver, I became a dangerous ditherer on the roads.'

People also feel vague and find it hard to concentrate. Many try to avoid driving as much as possible. However, if they are subject to sudden mood swings or bursts of anger they may throw caution to the winds and drive very dangerously.

I used to drive like a maniac – really fast and revved up. I had no concept of the flow of traffic. I had two accidents while I was coming off my pills.

I was always a sharp driver but in withdrawal I was erratic. I was speeding because it bothered me being stuck in traffic. I didn't like being trapped at the lights, so I would try to get through them on the yellow. I knew I was doing the wrong thing but I still did it. I often thought that if the authorities knew what I was doing they would have taken away my license. I sometimes see people doing the sorts of things I did and I wonder if they are on benzos or coming off them.

I used to drive machines. I used to drive trucks and double-decker buses in England. Now I'm dead scared to get in that little car.

I started to lose my confidence in heavy traffic or if I had to go over a bridge. In early withdrawal, I used to 'kangaroo' the delivery van along because I would get mixed up. Judging the speed of traffic was hard, so I would sit behind another car for ages if I needed to pass. I didn't feel I had enough strength in my body to put the brake on hard enough. Driving was a nightmare but I needed to do it for my job. It took several years to get better. Now I can drive absolutely anywhere again – it is second nature to me.

Benzodiazepine Brand Names

Brand name	Chemical name	Use
Almazine	lorazepam	medium-acting anxiolytic
Anxon	ketazolam	long-acting anxiolytic
Atensine	diazepam	long-acting anxiolytic
Ativan	lorazepam	medium-acting anxiolytic
Benzotran	oxazepam	short-acting anxiolytic
Centrax	prazepam	long-acting anxiolytic
Dalmane	flurazepam	long-acting hypnotic
Diazemuls	diazepam	long-acting anxiolytic (injection only)
Dormicum	nitrazepam	long-acting hypnotic
Dormonoct	loprazolam	hypnotic
Ducene	diazepam	long-acting anxiolytic
Euhypnos	temazepam	medium-acting hypnotic
Euhypnos Forte	temazepam	medium-acting hypnotic
Evacalm	diazepam	long-acting anxiolytic
Frisium	clobazam	long-acting anxiolytic
Halcion	triazolam	very short-acting hypnotic
Hypnodorm	flunitrazepam	long-acting hypnotic
Hypnovel	midazolam	intravenous anxiolytic
Lexotan	bromazepam	medium-acting anxiolytic
Librax	chlordiazepoxide	antispasmodic

Brand name contd.	Chemical name contd.	Use contd.
Librium	chlordiazepoxide	long-acting anxiolytic
Loramet	lometazepam	medium-acting hypnotic
Mogadon	nitrazepam	long-acting hypnotic
Murelax	oxazepam	short-acting anxiolytic
Nitepam	nitrazepam	long-acting hypnotic
Nitrados	nitrazepam	long-acting hypnotic
Nobrium	medazepam	long-acting anxiolytic
Noctamid	lomatazepam	medium-acting hypnotic
Normison	temazepam	medium-acting hypnotic
Oxanid	oxazepam	short-acting anxiolytic
Pro-pam	diazepam	long-acting anxiolytic
Rivotril	clonazepam	long-acting anti-convulsant, anxiolytic
Rohypnol	flunitrazepam	long-acting hypnotic
Sedapam	diazepam	long-acting anxiolytic
Serenid Forte	oxazepam	short-acting anxiolytic
Serenid-D	oxazepam	short-acting anxiolytic
Serenid	oxazepam	short-acting anxiolytic
Serepax	oxazepam	short-acting anxiolytic
Solis	diazepam	long-acting anxiolytic
Somnite	nitrazepam	long-acting hypnotic
Stesolid	diazepam	long-acting anxiolytic
Surem	nitrazepam	long-acting hypnotic
Tensium	diazepam	long-acting anxiolytic
Tranxene	clorazepate	long-acting anxiolytic
Tropium	chlordiazepoxide	long-acting anxiolytic
Unicomnia	nitrazepam	long-acting hypnotic
Valium	diazepam	long-acting anxiolytic
Valrelease	diazepam	long-acting anxiolytic
Xanax	alprazolam	medium-acting anxiolytic